IN THE WAKE OF THE GODS

IN THE
WAKE OF THE GODS

ON THE WATERWAYS OF IRELAND

HUGH MALET

1970
CHATTO & WINDUS
LONDON

Published by
Chatto & Windus Ltd
42 William IV Street
London, W.C.2

*

Clarke, Irwin & Co. Ltd
Toronto

SBN 7011 1533 5

Printed in Great Britain by
Cox & Wyman Ltd., London
Fakenham and Reading

For
Phoebe Jane
Grenville Malet

As this book is mainly about islands and lakes it will be a help to the general reader to know that the Gaelic for island is *Inis*, which is sometimes elided to *Inch*, as in Inchmore. The Gaelic for a lake should really be *Loch*, as in Scotland's Loch Lomond, but I have retained the Irish *Lough* because it is spelt this way on all the maps and is still in general use.

At the end of this book will be found the detailed acknowledgements to those who helped us so generously during our voyage, and in my later historical and archaeological researches.

CONTENTS

ILLUSTRATIONS

MAPS

The maps were drawn by Peter Beddoe. For detailed navigation among the islands the prevalence of rocks and shoals make it important to obtain charts whenever it is possible to do so.

IRISH LAKES AND WATERWAYS

Tory Island

Lough Swilly

Rathlin Island

Lough Foyle

NORTH CHANNEL

COLERAINE

Aran Mor

BURTONPORT

Rutland Island

River Bann

LONDONDERRY

SAINT'S WAY NORTH

ATLANTIC OCEAN

Lough Beg

Belfast Lough

Little Lough Derg

White Island

LOWER LOUGH ERNE

Lough Neagh

BELFAST

Ballyshannon

Dam

Killadeas

River Lagan

Inishmurray

Devenish

ENNISKILLEN

Strangford Lough

SLIGO

LOUGH GILL

UPPER LOUGH ERNE

Crom Castle

ULSTER CANAL

NEWRY

Lough Allen

Lough Arrow

BALLINAMORE CANAL

NEWRY CANAL

Lough Conn

Lough Key

BELTURBET

Lough Gara

Boyle

Carrick-on-Shannon

LOUGH OUGHTER

Clare Island

Lough Boderg

Lough Bofin

Inishturk

Carnadoe Waters

Lough Forbes

IRISH SEA

Inishbofin

Lanesborough

Richmond Harbour

Ballynahinch Lough

Lough Carra

LOUGH REE

Lough Owel

ROYAL CANAL

Lambay Isl

Lough Mask

Inchmore

MULLINGAR

SAINT'S WAY WEST

Cong Canal

Inner Lakes

Lough Corrib

ATHLONE

Ireland's

GALWAY

Clonmacnoise

EDENDERRY

DUBLIN

SAINT'S WAY SOUTH

GRAND CANAL

Shannon Harbour

GLENDALOUGH

Aran Islands

River Shannon

Athy

Holy Island

LOUGH DERG

Killaloe

Carlow

Dam

BARROW NAVIGATION

Kilkenny

LIMERICK

Shannon Estuary

Scattery Island

River Nore

Blasket Island

Killarney

Lough Leane

River Blackwater

River Suir

New Ross

WEXFORD

CORK

WATERFORD

Little Island

Saltee Islands

ST. GEORGE'S CHANNEL

Skellig Rocks

ATLANTIC OCEAN

0   10   20   30   40   50 miles

BEDDO

Chapter 1

THE WAY OF THE SAINTS

As the bow of the *Mary Ann* bit into the short steep waves of the upper Shannon and spray whipped back in our faces we caught our first brief glimpse of the islands. Imagine a view of the open sea stretching away to the far horizon but broken occasionally by rounded coasts and archipelagos, and you have some conception of the size of Lough Ree. Ahead of us lay the Way of the Saints, an immense galaxy of lakes winding away to Little Lough Derg in Donegal, and clustered with islands, some of them still inhabited. On lower Lough Erne lay the mysterious Druid sanctuary of White Island with the archaeological secrets of its sculptured gods.

Although our boat had a fair turn of speed for her size there was not sufficient time to explore every green-clad island along the Saints' Way during the few remaining months of summer, but we hoped to cover the length of the three navigations and visit the most important places. Our search was for the people who now live, or had once lived, on or around these lakes, the gods that they worshipped, the statues they carved, and the monasteries, round towers and castles which they built. We hoped also to discover what kind of people they were; something of the faiths and frailties, legends and ideals of the Druids, saints and heroes who once sailed these waters. We knew that a remarkable civilization had preserved the light of learning in Ireland during the Dark Ages, but we wondered what roots it had sprung from and what traces, what clues still lingered on the cropped green turf.

Our boat was manned, if that is the right phrase, by my wife Kay and myself, while our equipment for tackling this formidable enterprise was far from sophisticated. We had brought an umbrella, two light camp chairs, a cooker and a tent, and it was this last item which aroused the most adverse and cynical comments before we left England. "A *tent*! In Ireland! You're

13

mad," they had said. Prophetic words indeed, which we were later to intone as an encouraging litany at moments when rain-water flooded in, cooking became impossible or we were desperately bailing waves out of the bilges.

Our boat, though she had too little freeboard for safety and leaked persistently, did have the virtue of drawing very little water and could creep into corners of the lakes which were inaccessible to most other craft. She was a curious blend of the practical and the impossible : the practical being the fifteen-foot hull of a rowing-boat, with a small cover on the bow, and the impossible a very old car engine converted to marine use. A distinguished Irish author once compared this jumble of wire and metal to a broken-down toasting machine on account of the clouds of blue smoke which issued from its casing but it had survived a marathon crossing of the British Isles two years earlier and was now merrily churning its ancient pistons once again. Though there was just sufficient room for us both behind this smoking inferno there was neither peace nor comfort.

After patching up the *Mary Ann* at Waterford in the far south we had travelled about half-way across Ireland and our objective was to take our boat from coast to coast. This, we thought, would give us a purpose – a target of the kind which those who set out in frail and uncomfortable vessels require to maintain their spirits through all vicissitudes.

The Way of the Saints consists of three separate watersheds, the Shannon which rises close to the Border and winds by innumerable lakes and islands down to the sea at Limerick, and the Erne which rises in Lough Gowna, seeps into the labyrinthine mazes of Lough Oughter and on through two vast lakes to greet the sea in Donegal Bay. Lastly there is the Western Way of the Saints, the Corrib Navigation, which flows from Lough Carra to join the Atlantic in Galway Bay. Such is the main lake district of Ireland, most of it within the borders of the ancient kingdom of Connaught where an average of one acre in every twenty lies under water.

$\cdot \qquad \cdot \qquad \cdot \qquad \cdot \qquad \cdot$

14

For rather more than four thousand years these watersheds of lakes and linking rivers have provided a comparatively safe and reliable transport system for the local people. On land there were early trackways, and when the main body of Celts arrived they cleared some roads, but these often ran through forests haunted by robbers, wolves and wild boar, so travellers soon acquired an understandable preference for water transport wherever it was available. Although there were a few rapids and occasional portages, the Shannon, Erne and Corrib were almost perfect natural navigations for the shallow draught cots and coraghs of those days. The islands were also particularly revered by the Druids as possessing a special sanctity and on them they carried out their sacrifices, learned their magic lore by heart and instructed their neophytes. They built huts surrounded by earthern forts called raths, and when the population overflowed the islands they constructed lake villages called crannogs. These were held together by an ingenious matting of reed weighted with earth and rocks, with wooden piling to hold it in, and were connected with the mainland by underwater causeways built so cunningly that only the initiated could wade across. The Celts were good sailors and liked living on lakes, for examples of these crannogs have been found in Switzerland, near Glastonbury and at other places in England and Wales.

Then, some time between A.D. 425 and 435 a British stranger landed near Wicklow whose life and example changed the entire course of Irish history. He came at the request of an increasing Christian population which required a bishop to supervise its activities and appointments. There is evidence that St. Patrick voyaged on the Shannon and Corrib as well as on Little Lough Derg, and in his wake came a host of other saints to found those monasteries of the Celtic Church which are the pride of the Irish waterways and are still so well preserved on many of the lake islands.

The first recorded Viking raid overwhelmed the monastery on Lambay Island, near Dublin in 795, and from then on the Norsemen, being skilled sailors, used the rivers as highways into the heart of the land, burning, enslaving and desecrating the churches. Inevitably the lake islands and monasteries suffered from their depredations even more than the rest of Ireland, and many a ravaged abbey was never occupied again, but remained to provide us with mute evidence of that vanished civilization. For a long time the waterways altered little but boating was in the Irishman's blood and the Lough Ree yacht club claims to be the second oldest in the British Isles.

Then came the canal builders to raise the monumental locks, excavate the cuttings, deepen the rivers and construct their magnificent quays and harbours. Work began on the Shannon about 1769 but some of the most remarkable engineering achievements followed the potato famine between 1846 and 1851 when labour became all too cheap.

For about 140 years the canals and waterways bore much of the nation's merchandise until road and rail took over. By 1960 many people thought that inland navigation was doomed to extinction but there followed a remarkable revival in yachting and hire cruisers, drawing many tourists to a land where water may be a mixed blessing, but certainly could be used as a national asset.

So much we already knew as we left Athlone astern and began to buck and swing over the steep waves of Lough Ree, but these were only the bare bones of the story and we were searching for those people and places which could bring the dry facts of history to life.

The boatmen in Athlone had warned us that with a high sea running, if we wished to reach Coosan intact we should steer straight up into the north-west to gain sufficient sea room to turn and run before the wind across the roughest reach. After plunging and slithering well beyond the Yellow Islands we swung the bow suddenly in the trough between two waves and allowed the long rollers to push us away to the east; our main fear now was that we might be pooped by the following sea. When we arrived at a point just south of Hare Island the waves seemed to rise and smite us from every angle until the *Mary Ann* lurched and bucked like a cart-horse pursued by a horde of angry bees. To the disinterested eyes of any pagan gods still brooding over those waters our plight must have seemed absurd. Every now and again the stern would vanish into a trough, leaving us both sitting in mid air with only a hand on the tiller to keep our balance, and then, as the next wave caught up we would come to roost again with a resounding and painful thump. In this chastisement by water there was no set pattern of wave succeeding wave, but only a mass of breakers all around, and though we shipped a good deal of water it was impossible to get down to the bilge to bail it out.

The lake was no place for a small boat that day and we were thankful when, after nearly two hours of storm, Coosan's kindly headland loomed up over the waves, with its promise of solid earth under our feet, and we swung and jolted in between the black and white buoys which guard the entrance to the inner lakes.

Just around the headland in the calm and sheltered waters of Killenure Lough we moored in the harbour by the trim flagstaff below Harry Rice's house. Harry was one of a small band of waterway enthusiasts who managed to keep the Shannon open to navigation when it was threatened by low bridges, but his greatest achievement was to chart these waters, going out in his boat year after year with lead and line and, aided by his family, cementing marker stakes on to the most dangerous rocks and shoals. We learned much from Harry and Cynthia Rice and spent many a pleasant evening with them after long days on the lake, listening to those delightful Irish tales which linger somewhere on the frontiers between myth and reality.

The Rices would sometimes compare their house to a railway refreshment-room for few days went by without new voyagers calling in to consult the man who charted the Shannon and served as a living encyclopedia of its history and legends. Harry was a brilliant talker, and like most outstanding conversationalists possessed a set repertoire which he practised constantly in the old Irish oral tradition, combining humour and satire with criticism and anecdote. Outwardly at least he appeared to be a firm believer in the existence of the Lough Ree monster and, aided by a liberal ration of his favoured blend of whiskey would recount blood-curdling tales of his encounters with this elusive creature which he seemed to have met most frequently in the dark when returning home from his charting expeditions. One was never quite certain how much of it he believed himself and how much he was encouraging a legend which would bring the more curious to sail his beloved Shannon, but he had a knack of convincing people, and many who came to scoff went away scratching their heads and wondering. Harry had been severely disabled while serving in India but had recovered sufficiently to be invalided home to build Dunrovin and the magnificent garden slanting down to windward of that green and tree-clad headland.

Moving on, we followed the line of reed eastward from Coosan Point, entered a canal beside Friar's Island and ran between green banks until the inner fastness of Coosan Lough gleamed up at us in the twilight and we moored in the peaceful harbour below Creaghduff House, alongside an old steamer called the *Seagull* with her slanting Edwardian smokestack, and a host of lesser yachts and cruisers. This was to be our home port for the next few weeks while we explored the lakes.

We were aching in every limb after our long trial by waves, but soon after we moored a schooner called the *Betwixt* cast anchor in the bay and we were invited aboard. Some claimed that this ship first became famous as a gun runner during the time of the troubles while others held that she was given to sailing herself around the lakes. A distinguished Dublin surgeon once chartered her without learning this curious characteristic and took her to Lough Derg where he and his party entered port for a vital replenishment of their alcoholic stock, leaving the *Betwixt* with her canvas still set and perhaps a trifle loosely moored. When they returned they discovered that she had vanished and as they scanned the far horizon they saw her disappearing into another harbour some six windy miles away. The party clambered into the nearest available boat and followed at full speed but as they drew near their quarry the *Betwixt* performed a series of neat tacks, without a soul aboard, went right about and came creaming past them at a full five knots, and it was not until they returned to the original port of call that they managed to recapture her.

In the warm and comfortable cabin of this venerable craft

we listened to a number of strange tales but the most memorable of them all was told by Walter Levinge.

"There lies," he said, "to the west of Lough Ree and a little way off the main road from Athlone to Roscommon, a lough called Funshinagh. For no apparent reason this lake, like a few more in western Ireland, runs completely dry every four or five years; the water drains away through a hole in the bottom as though a plug had been pulled out of a bath. Some claim that it falls through hidden caves to the sea though no one is really certain, but as it goes it leaves behind a host of dying perch and pike and rudd floundering on its bed. These fish are regarded as rare delicacies by the local pigs which are turned loose to feed on them.

"I have seen," he said, "a pig with its legs sunk deep in the mud and a live six-foot eel wound round and round its neck while it chewed happily away at the tail end!"

At length we clambered down into the dinghy. A moon as broad and round as a prosperous farmer's face peered down at us from a silver sky fringed with a rim of cloud on the far horizon. The tall reed which skirts most of the inner lakes rose like a hosting of spears above our heads and the oars dipped gently into the dark water. The night stillness was broken only by the tinkle of drops tumbling from the blades, combining with the steady beat of a mallard's wings sounding up from the darkness beyond Thatch Island; its shadow was silhouetted briefly against the stars before it turned and headed out towards Lough Ree.

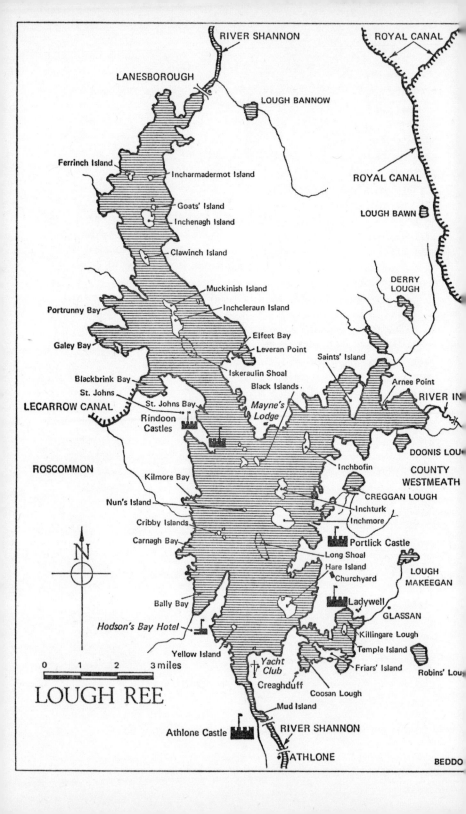

Chapter 2

THE ISLANDERS

T HE morning dawned fine and the wind had dropped so I set out alone to seek the islanders, pointing the bow of the *Mary Ann* north through Coosan and Killenure on to the broad expanse of Lough Ree. Kay had returned to Waterford to collect our car. In contrast to the previous week the water was absolutely still. Even on the most breathless day a salt sea has about it some slight swell or hint of movement but on Ree a spell had been cast and the surface spread out, placid, clear and fragile as a rounded mirror which it seemed a desecration to disturb.

Grateful for this rest from the rollers I steered north past Hare Island, Inchmore and Inchturk, every now and again consulting the charts carefully for fear that I might run aground on the shoals which crop up here and there among these islands. Gradually Inchbofin loomed closer and as I rounded the southern point I saw a man studying the boat through a pair of binoculars.

Pat Connell came down to the shore to take the mooring line and told me that his two brothers were away fishing on Lough Gara, for the family lived mainly from what they could catch in the lakes. Sometimes they use nets, at other times long lines which may reach for three or four miles and are baited at intervals. Setting this tackle right across the lakes could, he said, be extremely arduous work in cold and windy weather. Though they take trout and salmon occasionally the catch is mostly pike, and eels which are kept alive in small square wooden boxes with breathing holes drilled in the lid and bottom to admit sufficient air and water. As soon as this has been half filled it is dropped into the shallows until a fixed day of the week – usually Thursday – when a buyer comes over the border from Enniskillen in Northern Ireland to purchase the catch, meeting the islanders at an appointed time and place on the mainland.

21

A family may well earn some £40 a week from their fishing if they are fortunate, but they make little enough in the winter and the quality of their catch is apt to vary. The eels are exported to England and to the Continent while some of the pike go, I was told later, to Paris where it is considered to be a greater delicacy than salmon; the British never seem to have mastered the art of cooking this fish with all the appropriate sauces, but the French have brought it to perfection.

Inchbofin is less than a mile long and as we passed the Connells' carefully planted garden we came to the small fields, rich and heavy with clover and studded with wild flowers. I could not avoid a feeling of wonder that any people in our present age could lead such an entirely independent existence in these remote surroundings.

"Being here and owning your own island," I said, "you can do just as you wish – no one controls your lives, and perhaps you're the last really free people left."

"Ah, yes," said Pat, "but it's so lonesome here. Many of our people have gone out of the country altogether."

Inchbofin must certainly be a very deserted place indeed when the winter gales sweep over those wide waters and cut the islanders off from the mainland for weeks at a time but on that pleasant summer afternoon with the sun burning down on our backs, the hedges blazing with colour and the lake water dappling the hull of the crazy wooden cattle boat, the winter seemed very far away and I recalled one definition of heaven as a bourne of boats and deep green islands set in summer seas.

The monastery lies near the northern promontory and on a warm summer day there is a hum of bees around the crumbling tracery of the windows, mingling with the rustling wind in the trees and the soft persistence of lake water lapping on the long shore. As the ruins are rarely visited even by the islanders themselves a variety of wildfowl come in close to feed and we could hear them only a few yards away, arguing indignantly with each other over the choicest morsels. Certainly the abbey was an extensive one and among the few lake island monasteries which continued to be occupied up to the late Middle Ages. I had decided to visit this place first, partly because there was a good deal of it still left standing, and partly because it was traditionally the earliest Christian foundation on Lough Ree.

Legend has it that Inchbofin was established by St. Patrick's two "nephews", St. Rioch and St. Germain. It is always a complicated task to disentangle the lives of the Celtic saints, since many had the same names and later chroniclers were never backward in adding a few tall stories of their own to liven matters up a little and garnish the barren facts of history, but it seems that St. Germain, having fulfilled his ministry on Inchbofin, moved on to the Isle of Man about 477, to become the first bishop there. He is still the patron saint of the church within the walls of Peel Castle in the parish which bears his name, and his feast day is July 3. Rioch seems to have had more of a vocation for the ascetic life for the tale goes that he fasted so long and remained so still that after forty-four years on the island the moss and grasses crept gradually over his skin and covered him in folds until there was practically nothing to be seen of him at all, a tale which clearly proves that the Celtic imagination was no less fertile fourteen centuries ago than it is today. Indeed, the art of remaining still is a gift which later ages seem to have lost and it may be that the legendary example of St. Rioch was intended to point a moral.

All that we know of Rioch as a person comes down to us from a miracle performed by another saint. One day a local warrior chieftain applied to the Church to be given a new face, which he sorely needed for he had the ugliest features that had ever been seen, frightening the children and turning the milk sour. After much preparation by way of fasting, penance and amendment of life he was at last deemed to be prepared for his metamorphosis and was asked to name the features that he would most like his own to resemble.

"Sure," he said, "and there's no one in the world I'd sooner look like than St. Rioch." In the twinkling of an eye there was a fine carbon copy of Rioch's features where before there had been nothing but gnarls, warts and protuberances, and one very much hopes that he received a modicum of Rioch's sanctity along with his physiognomy, for as we shall see, the ethics of some of those early Irish warriors left a certain amount to be desired.

Of the two remaining churches on Inchbofin the larger was cruciform, and among the island monasteries comparable only in size with St. Mary's Abbey at Devenish on Lough Erne. It is an unusual blend of what I guessed to be tenth and fourteenth century architectures while a large room which may have been a dormitory stands over a lower dwelling, possibly a refectory, on the north-western side. On an outer wall we found a gem of a small Romanesque window near a later tracery window crowned by a well-preserved and finely carved head of a man with a beard and a conical helmet, similar to those across the lake at Hodson's Bay Hotel. Pat Connell told me that this was definitely a portrait of Rioch himself and though the workmanship is of about the fourteenth century the statement was a valuable confirmation of Rioch's association with the island.

Now if Rioch was St. Patrick's librarian it is a pleasant speculation that the patron saint may have visited Inchbofin from time to time. Both belonged to the Celtic Church which was the missionary outcome of the faith which had evolved under Roman rule in Britain. Though Protestant and Roman Catholic scholars have sought to claim it as their own the Celtic Church was really the common ancestor of both denominations in these islands, for relics were venerated, communion was given in both kinds and some of its priests were married. It was generally centred on Armagh and Cashel but many of its theological colleges and monasteries were built along the islands and shores of the Saints' Way where much of the population had been settled since Druid times, communications were excellent and fish for fast days could be caught swiftly and served up fresh. Devenish, Lisgoole, Holy Island, Clonmacnois, Inchagoill (on Lough Corrib) and Inchcleraun on Lough Ree were all once important centres of learning, though these were only a few of the main abbeys which sprang up along these winding waterways.

St. Patrick was unique in being not only one of the humblest and kindest of men, but also one of the very few who ever managed to organize a considerable number of Irishmen with any permanent effect, and has consequently earned their undying veneration. Professor Hanson's scholarly study of Patrick has entirely swept away the earlier concept of a commanding and demanding, perpetually miracle-working prelate, and replaced it with a far gentler, more humble and more genuine figure.

It is now clear that Patrick came most probably from Somerset, Dorset or Devon, that he was sent to Ireland by the Celtic Church in Britain, that he never visited France, or Gaul as it was then called, that he probably never wrote the famous hymn now called the *Breastplate*, and that most of the corpus of miracles attributed to him is clearly an incrustation of myth – the garnishings of later writers who were more intent on venerating the saint and his achievement than recounting the true historical details.

In place of that outworn vision of an overbearing prelate which we may call the Patrician cultus there emerges an infinitely more fascinating character who was extremely anxious not to give offence and constantly struggled to save his Church from persecution in a still largely Druidical land. About 406 he had been captured by Irish pirates at his family's comfortable country villa and sold into slavery to tend sheep in a wood called Foclut which was probably on the borders of Sligo and Mayo not so very far from Inchagoill Island on Lough Corrib, where as we shall find later a church is dedicated to him and a very ancient standing stone to his reputed skipper, Lugnaedon.

Escaping from his Druid master Patrick made his way across some 200 miles of country, embarked with a crew of sailors who may well have been pirates, and returned after many privations to his family in Britain. His traumatic enslavement had bred a deep faith but his lost childhood had left him educationally very backward, so he studied, possibly at Glastonbury, to acquire sufficient learning to become one of those priests whose ministry is based more on their experience of life than on their intellectual ability, for as he wrote in his own touchingly halting Latin :

I am Patrick, a sinner, most unlearned, the least of all the faithful and utterly despised by many.

25

I was like a stone lying in the deep mire; and He that is mighty came and in His mercy lifted me up, and raised me aloft, and placed me on the top of the wall.

It was very understandable that the British should have been anxious to convert the pagan Irish who were raiding their coasts at that time, and Patrick was consecrated and returned as a missionary bishop to the land where once he had been enslaved. We do not really know how long he stayed there or even whether he was buried there, but we do know that his was not the triumphal episcopate once envisaged but rather a period of hard labour and total insecurity, while on his itineraries and inland voyages he lived in daily expectation of murder, poisoning, betrayal or captivity – in other words he belonged to what was still largely the Christian underground, despite the many conversions already made from Whithorn Abbey and from the trading posts on the eastern coast. On one occasion he was clapped in irons and imprisoned for fourteen days, possibly in one of those pits reserved for prisoners of war, criminals, delinquent hostages and runaway slaves.

The Druids were Patrick's chief opponents and it is sun-worship alone which receives a specific trouncing in the *Confession* which he wrote in his old age :

For this sun which we see rises daily for us because he commands so, but it will never reign, nor will its splendour last; what is more, those wretches who adore it will be miserably punished.

Inevitably a vast incrustation of myths and legends evolved around Patrick's achievement, and one of the most delightful tells how he set out for Tara to convert the pagans there but learned that an ambush would be laid for him by the Druids, so he composed his famous hymn called the *Deer's Cry* or *Breastplate*, for protection. As the bishop and his monks approached the ambush they sang out the verses with their invocation to the Trinity combining with strong traces of Druidical worship:

I bind unto myself today
The virtues of the star-lit heaven,
The glorious sun's life-giving ray,
The whiteness of the moon at even,
The flashing of the lightning free,
The whirling wind's tempestuous shocks,
The stable earth, the deep salt sea
Around the old eternal rocks.

And the spell worked, for all that the waiting warriors saw passing by was a herd of wild deer with a fawn following behind; thus, it was said, did the saint and his companions escape unscathed.

With the sun glinting down through the leaves and the murmur of bees combining with the tapping of water along the shore I recalled the strange experience of a man who had visited this ruin on Inchbofin some 500 years after the last of the monks had been driven from it. One fine sunny afternoon he and his brother had moored their boat by the trees and had come ashore for a picnic. They were sitting under the monastery walls after their meal when they heard distinctly, from somewhere quite close at hand, the sound of monks singing the *appropriate office* for the hour. The gentle intonation of the plain chant lasted less than a minute but far from filling them with fear it left them with a deep sense of peace and tranquillity and a pleasant memory which they have long treasured.

As Pat and I walked back across the island the Connell's terrier, Daisy, circled around us chasing rabbits and birds through the hedges and barking until we reached the house where Mrs. Connell offered me crisp, warm home-baked bread which was not long out of the oven.

"Sure and I don't know what those English girls are doing all the time, dusting about, and this and that! When I have seven men in here for the haymaking what would I do if I had to buy the bread for them?"

There would be two ways of buying bread from Inchbofin.

One would be to take a boat a mile or so to the mainland and walk or bicycle some ten miles to Athlone, the only place at which it would be generally available, or alternatively one could row about seven miles straight across the lake, always assuming that the weather was favourable. Either way it would be a major operation and when the islanders do their shopping, which is generally on Saturdays, they have to make very certain that nothing is forgotten.

I wended my way back, keeping to the east of the islands, well sheltered from the prevailing wind and by the time that I had rounded the Napper Rocks and was off Holly Point a long swell was running and a gale rising out of a black horizon to chase the *Mary Ann* to her haven beyond the tall reeds in Coosan Lough.

Chapter 3

THE DRUIDS

THE following day we went in search of a very different kind of islander. Charlie Backhouse was then well over eighty and had come to Ireland more than forty years before, carrying a loaded revolver at the bottom of his suitcase as an aid to self-defence in those troubled times. Far from being shot at he was made very welcome, and settled down for the rest of his life at Athlone, where he gradually fell under the spell of the lakes and islands. In England he had been mainly employed as an actor and had known the golden days of the Edwardian music-halls, but though born and bred a Londoner he soon took to himself two islands. The first of these was Mud Island which lies in the neck of the Shannon just above Athlone and was merely a heap of soil and stones dredged out of the depths and piled on one side when the river was being made navigable, about 1837, to supersede the canal which by-passed the town rapids.

Charlie's other island we never managed to discover, but it lay hidden deep in some bay in the upper reaches of the lake; a place utterly remote from the prying eyes of mankind, with a concrete block which he had built for keeping a dry and firm base under his tent.

To Mud Island Charlie brought one of the Englishman's greatest talents – his skill as a gardener. He turned his tiny kingdom into a place of great beauty with hollyhocks rioting over it and roses bursting into a blaze of colour around the carefully marshalled flower-beds, while the mud once dredged from the river proved extraordinarily fertile. With his small attaché-case for carrying provisions to his boat Charlie became a familiar figure in the town and earned his living as a typographer with the Athlone Press. As he walked to and from his work the children would cluster about him, for he would distribute a largesse of sweets and chocolates as he went his way.

There is about those who choose the solitary life a certain

29

quality which intrigues us and so we set out the following day to seek the hermit of Mud Island and discover the less remote of his two sanctuaries. Once again it was a windy, boisterous day with white crests of waves chasing each other across the lake and a grey, streaky sky with a few seagulls whirling across it like white leaves torn away on the wind. "I don't think it'll be *wicked* out there today," Walter Levinge had said in reply to my anxious inquiry, and as we bucked and rolled and wallowed in the breakers off Hare Island we vowed that we would on no account venture out when it was wicked, but at last we slipped past Carberry Island into the sheltered waters above Athlone.

There lay Mud Island, a few hundred yards above the railway bridge and well within sight of the town. Roses had rioted over the battered remnants of a crumbling greenhouse, and an ancient barge had been floated up on the northern beach.

As we turned out of the main pull of the current I felt the need to give some warning of our approach, but my voice faded away unanswered on the wind. The entire island was only some sixty yards across and the barge which had so long been Charlie's home listed gently, reflecting sunshine from the door and from glass windows cut in the hull. It was anchored securely, but not, one felt, so firmly that the huge power of the flooded river might not one day sweep it away altogether, and I was told that its owner had spent many an anxious night in it wondering whether his last hour had come while the waters swirled past and the old tub ground restlessly at her moorings.

The interior of the barge was empty save for a narrow iron bed and a terracotta cross hanging from a bracket on the bulwark, but as I walked down the centre of the garden island I felt that I was being watched. A Shannon rowing-boat had been pulled up well above the waterline and an ancient cabin cruiser, the *Panama*, battered and patched but still sturdy, swung at anchor off the south headland.

There was a dark corner of the greenhouse where roses had tangled over the roof and as I glanced in there loomed out what appeared to be the face of the Devil himself, seemingly suspended in mid air and crowned by two sharp horns. Doubtless the worthy saints who sailed the Shannon in centuries past would have regarded such an apparition as a perfectly normal everyday occurrence, but since the fiend has nowadays grown subtler in his disguises I was momentarily at a loss for the correct words of exorcism. My surprise was replaced by suspicion when the apparition gave out a low, hoarse growl, but it was not until I had moved out of the sunlight that the fiend vanished and his place was taken by a handsome and terrestrial but rather fierce-looking boxer dog with his ears pricked up expectantly. We never did manage to meet the hermit of Mud Island for he died in hospital at the ripe old age of eighty-four, but his dog was properly cared for.

Each one of the Shannon lakes has its own atmosphere but few are subject to such a vast variety of sudden changes as Lough Ree, with its thousand and one different moods. Sometimes it is full of strange lights and mystical and still, sometimes it is a seething mass of breaking waves and at other times it is cloaked in a white covering of mist. These are the principal moods of this lake, but there are infinite variations as we discovered the next day when we sailed past Hare Island. There was no breath of wind but only a strange glitter on the surface which was filled with an extraordinary series of mirages and reflections. A white yacht far away beyond the Long Shoal seemed to be floating six feet above the water, the islands appeared to be suspended in mid air and a group of white swans which had come to rest on the jagged and dangerous Hexagon shoal looked as though the laws of gravity had ceased to apply to them since they were apparently hanging motionless some twenty feet up in the sky. From a larger boat it is possible that one might not encounter the extraordinary phenomenon of these lake mirages, which are more varied than those of the desert, but they bring one perhaps a little closer to comprehending the visionary element in the Irish character.

As we rounded Inchmore we saw the low, wooded outline of Nun's Island, the most central of them all, rising out of the deepest part of the lake.

To avoid the reef on the eastern coast we stopped the engine and paddled gently and cautiously in past the rocks to a mooring in deep water. Like the lakes, each island has its own distinctive character and the few people I met who knew it all had the same question to ask of this one – "Don't you think it's a strange, almost *haunted* place?" they would say.

We agreed that there was something very weird about Nun's Island. There clings to it an atmosphere of pre-history as though, four miles from the nearest shore and nearly a mile from any other island it had been left behind, like Conan-Doyle's Lost World, when the rest of evolution had moved on. Through over 100 feet of murky water the very deepest parts of the lake plunge away on either side and there are many who hold that some kind of antediluvian creature similar to the Loch Ness monster still lurks under these bleak wastes. The first record of its appearance in Ree comes from a twelfth-century chronicler, which is admittedly a far from reliable source, but the latest is provided by three priests who were fishing off the island recently. Had it been only one of the reverend gentlemen one might be tempted to suggest that he had suffered a slight optical illusion but three would seem to offer evidence which would be harder to contest. I saw a drawing which they had made of the creature and it did indeed resemble the aquatic beasts which have been sighted in the lakes and open sea around Scotland.

Though the islanders deny any knowledge of a monster they did tell me of a large mammal which they call the *white cow* which they have caught in their nets from time to time. With a powerful rip and a spouting of water it would slash through two thick strands of mesh, leaving a hole up to about six feet wide. In the *Life of St. Mochua of Balla* is the tale of a wounded stag which took refuge on an unnamed island in Lough Ree. The chase drew up at the brink, for all the huntsmen knew that the monsters which infested the lake would destroy anyone who swam in it. At length a man was persuaded to take the risk; he reached the island safely and dispatched the deer, but on the way back the creature in the water seized him and he vanished for ever.

Though it is just feasible that monsters as vicious as crocodiles, and perhaps not greatly dissimilar did once lurk in these lakes, there is no indication that any remaining aquatic animals are of the man-eating species; on the contrary, if they do exist, they would seem to be remarkably peaceful and elusive, and definitely in the reluctant dragon class.

In Irish folklore a curious similarity runs through the descriptions of these monsters, which helps to make one perhaps a little more convinced of some kind of biological origin. They are generally covered with short hair over their hides and a mane at the nape; large jaws with protruding teeth and a serpent-like motion in the water is common to them all, but myth does not confine them entirely to the lakes for ancient legends constantly locate them in deep wells, mountain caves and the lonely and deserted ruins of castles.

Although these monsters are more likely to be related to the turtle than to the serpent they do have a visual resemblance to exceptionally large eels. According to popular belief they should therefore have been banished from the country when St. Patrick, after a long spell of fasting and prayer, gathered all the venomous creatures, demons and serpents together on top of Croagh Patrick Mountain and herded them into the sea down a deep gulley called the *Hollow of the Demons*. In common with so much mythology there is a hard basis of fact in the patron saint's spiritual achievement, but the snake side of the story is entirely fictitious and was probably the invention of a character called Jocelin in the twelfth century, for several classical writers had commented on Ireland's snakelessness more than a thousand years earlier. I once came across a holy painting of exceptionally powerful colouring for sale in a remote Arab market in Africa – depicting the saint in full canonical robes, a commanding hand pointing to the sea while the creatures slithered past him to their fate – a reminder of the Irishman's unique gift for telling the kind of tall stories which travel all around the globe.

What Patrick banished from the land was not the snake but the *symbol* of the snake depicted in the earliest Celtic art as held in the left hand of Cernunnos, the witch god of fertility. This was the deity whose carving we were to find later, lurking by the shore of Boa Island on Lower Lough Erne.

Whether turtle or serpent the Lough Ree monster has not been considered carnivorous and is supposed to live on water weeds and lilies, which is the reason why it has been suggested in various uninhibited quarters that it ought to be captured and bred by British Waterways and C.I.E. to keep down the weed along their more neglected navigations.

Although we scanned the lake diligently around Nun's Island we saw no sign of the familiar protruding neck and hump with the spikes on top, and eased the boat through the last few feet of translucent water and stepped ashore. Clouds of terns, the swallows of the sea as they are sometimes called, came tumbling and wheeling over our heads, screaming at our intrusion, for this island is in a traditionally rough part of the lake where there are seldom more than a few visiting fishermen during the brief dapping season.

At one time the owner, Mr James Tiernan, who lives on neighbouring Inchmore tried to graze cattle on Nun's Island; he would take them over in the afternoon and they might stay for a night or so, but invariably they would swim away to some less haunted island soon afterwards. On one occasion the skipper of a passing barge sighted these aqueous cattle well out to sea and heading in a direction which would have involved more miles of swimming than they could have managed. At first he feared that he had sighted the monster but when he realized that they were ordinary cows he managed to lasso their heads and tow them to the nearest mainland where the owner was able to recover his herd.

The jungle of briars and blackthorn was so thick that we never penetrated beyond a small circular field in the centre and by that time were bleeding so profusely from the thorns that we abandoned the search for the church, but the last person I met who had managed to reach it told me that he had discovered a mallard nesting on the grey stone altar.

The area around is not a specified bird sanctuary, but was then a natural one. We had never seen a place where gulls, terns, mallard, guillemot and cormorants nested side by side on open banks and ledges of rock with no apparent effort at concealment. We found the nest of a Greater Crested Grebe with one of the newly hatched chicks pushing its small, vividly coloured head high into the air. These birds are still quite numerous on Lough Ree and often as we were scanning for hidden snags and shoals their heraldic heads would emerge distractingly from the water, for they are divers and can remain under for a long time. They have about them the straight-necked imperious gaze of Victorian ladies distressed at some minor infringement of etiquette.

At the far end of the island, perched on a rock, was the inevitable cormorant with his wings hung out to dry, black, hunched and prehistoric. Another flew low over our heads. Yet another came skimming across the water, its beak and neck stretched out like a warhead and giving the sinister impression of a rocket impelled by direct, purposeful and uncomplicated flight. Cormorants alarm one by their intentness and add to the island's air of survival from some period of pre-history if possible even more savage and starkly ferocious than our own. The almost impenetrable jungle of dark blackthorn lends the place a more sombre colouring than the other islands and leaves one with an awed feeling of the briefness of human achievement against the immense background of biological evolution.

To avoid grave robbers and to prevent the corpses from being dug up by wild animals, Nun's Island was used for many thousands of years to bury the dead. It was not surprising that the Druidic religion attached a special sanctity to islands of any kind, because dead souls, it was held, could not cross over water and later it was believed that certain saints of the Celtic Church possessed spiritual powers which would aid the resurrection of those lesser mortals who were buried around them. Every inch of Nun's Island that is not rock must have been turned over again and again to inter new bodies, for the soil is still full of skulls and bones. The corpses of those who dwelt on the mainland were laid out on a huge slab of stone which can be seen near Portlick Castle, and after a while came the kind of funeral barge described in "The Passing of Arthur" as "Dark as a funeral scarf from stem to stern," to carry the bier away:

> *To the island-valley of Avilion;*
> *Where falls not hail, or rain, or any snow*
> *Nor ever wind blows loudly . . .*

And there would be the same keening as that of the three queens who took the dying king away:

> A cry that shiver'd to the tingling stars,
> And, as it were once voice, an agony
> Of lamentation, like a wind that shrills
> All night in a waste land, where no one comes
> Or hath come, since the making of the world.

Unlike the humans the many gulls and terns and diving birds have no burial, and we found their bones and feathers littered along the shore. Even the living birds were so unused to strangers that one could touch their nests before they flew away.

Carefully avoiding another submerged reef we travelled north for just over a mile and ground the keel gently into the half-moon-shaped beach of King's Island which, in stark contrast, was almost devoid of trees or bushes of any kind. It was quite small and rose sharply from the water to a plateau where there was a broad "street" with some six or seven houses facing each other across the grassy sward. The two main families on this island were the Hanleys and the O'Haras and not many years ago every house was full of children and every chimney smoking, but when we called the population had shrunk to one woman and a boy who were away shopping on the mainland; their dog was at first suspicious and gave a few perfunctory barks but eventually came close enough to establish diplomatic relations with the foreigners.

The Hanley family are the hereditary stewards of the very ancient crozier and bell of St. Berach who was reputedly born on February 15, in the year 521. After Berach had been baptized his mother naturally wished to keep him in her care, but his uncle, St. Freoch said "let me have the bringing up of this little one; God will provide for his sustenance", and this materialized, it was said, in due course in the form of honey from the lobe of Freoch's ear, which enabled the child to be reared from that time on in an entirely ecclesiastical environment. In due course Berach founded his own abbey at Termonbarry or Termon Berach some seven miles up river from Lough Ree where the Royal Canal now locks down into the Shannon.

About thirty years ago the family handed the crozier over to the safe keeping of the Royal Irish Academy and it can now be seen in the National Museum in Dublin. Barry, derived from Berach, is often used as a Christian name in local families and in others related to them wherever the Irish have settled around the world.

As a young wandering monk Berach, it was said, called in one hot summer day at the hall of Bregha King of Tara. The building was generously lined with fifty vats of beer waiting for a roisterous evening of feasting but the steward refused to allow the saint so much as half a cup to stop his thirst and sent Berach on his way. Soon afterwards the King returned equally thirsty from hunting and asked for a beaker of ale, but when they went to draw they found that every vat was empty though not the slightest drop had been spilt. The royal wrath descended on the steward, who racked his brains until he remembered the visitor.

"There did come to us," he said at length, "a student with a little bell and staff, and asked for a drink in the name of the Lord, and it was refused him."

"Take horses and go after him quickly, wheresoever he be overtaken," cried the thirsty King, "and let no violence be done to him, but let him be adjured in the name of the Lord and he will come back."

When Berach was found the King prostrated himself before him, the saint made the sign of the cross with bell and staff over the vats, and when the lids were opened there was better beer in them than ever there had been before. Whether the saint stayed on to dine is a matter not recorded by the chroniclers but the King did give him his own suit of clothes and sent him a new one every year, so presumably the moral of the tale is that we should not judge people by the clothes they wear but rather by the personality behind their outward appearance.

That evening we pitched our tent in a small clearing cut for us by Pat Duffy between the harbour and the ruined church founded by St. Ciaran on Hare Island. In our exploration of these lakes our daily routine was simple though it could be extremely arduous, particularly if the weather was unfavourable. We would select an interesting or picturesque island as a headquarters and set up camp in a reasonably sheltered clearing, always well away from any cattle. In inhabited places we invariably asked local people where they would like us to be, for one can still cause offence in Ireland by desecrating the fairy knoll with one's midnight presence. Humping the tent and kit up from our mooring was a burdensome task, so we seldom encamped far from the boat – it was in any case our sole means of escaping from uninhabited islets so that we had to be well within range of the *Mary Ann* in case a storm blew up.

From each temporary base we sought to cover as wide an area of water as possible to avoid the time-wasting burden of moving camp and kit, but eventually our lines of communication would become so extended that we would have to search for a new headquarters. Carrying a gas cooker was out of the question in a small boat which was constantly being thrown about by waves, so we used a Primus which coped with coffee, eggs and soup reasonably quickly and for larger meals we had a pressure cooker which functioned best on a wood or turf fire. We were far too busy to attempt any exotic dishes and bread, cheese and chocolate with a glass of cider was the staple diet of our midday meal. All our cooking had to be done on land and in the open since there was no room on the boat.

I liked to make a fire in the evening if I could find wood or turf, for though the smoke had a maddening habit of following us round wherever we sat the evenings could be cool and a crackling blaze was comforting under the lonely vastness of those lakeside nights. We lived indeed very much like the earliest voyagers on these broad navigations, and if there were grim and rainy days there were also exhilarating hours when the water sparkled with refracted sunlight and the breezes from the rich island pastures came down laden with the scent of clover.

Though the wood was a little damp that evening on Hare Island we soon had a good fire blazing with plenty of hot ash in the centre where the pressure cooker hummed gently, giving out a tantalizing smell of Irish stew.

Then we were off to explore the island which is perhaps half a mile across by rather more than a half-mile from north to south. The Lodge in the centre is an attractive Victorian Gothic building with a large light drawing-room and outbuildings at the side, while the only other habitation is a small cottage on the south-west coast with a few of those apple trees growing around it which the Druids held in such high veneration. Behind the main house stretches the broad crescent of a deep and sheltering oak wood and as we moved into it we caught a glimpse of the increasingly rare red squirrel which had found a brief sanctuary there against the invasions of the grey menace.

The broad columns of the oak boles and the interlacing branches rustling in the wind high above our heads carried our thoughts back to the pagan seats of learning which were once centred on these islands. Though some scholars associate the word Druid with various Aryan terms for an oak tree I prefer the derivation from the root words *dru-*, meaning *very*, and *vid-*, meaning knowing, which suggests that they were considered to be very knowing, or *very wise* men. This is partly supported by Diodorus, a contemporary of Julius Caesar who wrote, "Some whom they call Druids, are very highly honoured as philosophers and theologians," and partly by St. Columba to whom is attributed the remark "Christ the Son of God is my Druid", by which he meant pattern and ensample. Although the Druids sacrificed and divined the future from the entrails of their victims they were not priests as we understand the term, but rather diviners, experts on ethics and magical lore, and teachers of the very important poetical sagas in which the legends of the gods and the history of the Celtic race was enshrined. They were rather more than mere witch-doctors or shamans, but Diodorus exaggerated a little when he called them philosophers and theologians. The mistletoe which grows on oaks and on apple trees was certainly one of their main herbs of power, but by no means the only one, and as I shall explain later their religious ritual evolved from a curious natural trinity.

They founded communities on these islands where the neophytes were initiated into the mysteries and magic ceremonies of the tribal religion and learned by heart the natural science, astronomy and mythological lore of their faith. The novice was subjected to a very long probationary period involving testing physical ordeals and much of this high standard of asceticism was inherited by the saints of the Celtic Church who, as we shall see, imposed almost intolerable strains on their physical endurance in order to attain the higher realms of spirituality.

Strictly speaking the word Druid should therefore be confined to that small section of ancient Celtic society which was concerned with these specialized functions, but the word is also used very loosely to cover the entire Celtic aristocracy centred around the court of each of the petty kings, for this was, as I hope to show, essentially a state religion. The term is therefore often used of poets, smiths, apothecaries, huntsmen, goldsmiths, charioteers and a host of other carefully graded occupations. These "courtiers" served a local King and believed in what we can call for want of a better term the Druidic religion; this was essentially a fertility cultus in which the gods had to be propitiated with sacrifices to ensure that they would grant mankind such varying needs as good crops, children and successful fishing. They also held that the human soul could not die but was born again into another body without very long delay – a process which we call the transmigration of souls – a concept rather more elevated than mere shape-shifting.

Any striking natural landmark – an island, a mountain, a river or a ravine was, they believed, especially hallowed, and Druidic worship was mainly local in its affiliations, although certain important gods called the Tuatha de Danann were worshipped throughout the land.

The least attractive feature of the cult was the human and animal sacrifices which were undertaken to propitiate the gods and ensure the fertility of all living things. It was not unreasonable that a people who held that the soul must be reborn almost immediately the body died should possess a low estimate of the value of human life, so that those who were sick or anxious to obtain some benefit would think little of burning a criminal, a captive or a child to obtain their ends; they would even sacrifice themselves.

There can be no doubt that sacrifices were carried out on most of these islands, since they were especially sacred to the Celtic religion, and the feast of Samain on November 1, was a particularly favoured time because it was felt that the power of

40

the warm gods of air and sunlight was waning, while the fearful authorities of sleet and the winter underworld were waxing in power. Hallowe'en, on October 31, still marks this pagan fire festival.

Druidic worship was really based on a deep respect, at times a fear, of those natural phenomena which men could not properly comprehend. It involved a varied pantheon but the leading deity in Ireland seems to have been that sun god whose worship Patrick so roundly condemned called Cenn Cruaich or Lord of the High Place, for the Celtic religion naturally centred around the sun as the giver of life, and the mysterious and beautiful moon:

> *Milk and corn*
> *Would they beg from him, swiftly,*
> *In return for a third of their healthy children:*
> *Great was the horror and the terror of him.*

So wrote the later monk who celebrated the legend of St. Patrick's courage when he strode up to the high place at Magh Slecht, near Lough Ballymagauran, close to the present Ballina-more Canal where, like the heathen idols of the Old Testament Cenn's figure crowned with beaten gold crouched, surrounded by twelve stone idols of the Celtic pantheon. According to the legend the saint belted this statue so hard with a sledge-hammer that he clove it from head to foot, but this does not square with what we now know of Patrick's character and it is much more likely that it was due to the saint's teaching and preaching that "Cenn of the many mists" began to wither away with all the evils, child sacrifices and libations of human blood associated with his cult. Moreover, Mr. Hugh Maguire, in a recent article has suggested that the figure still stands not very far from the original site. But pagan practices continued and it was many centuries before the Celtic Church and its successors were able to expunge the scent of burning flesh from the high places and remote lakeside groves of Ireland.

It was in order to crush this Druidical influence and re-place it with a nobler ethic that St. Ciaran came to Hare Island about the year 541, carrying his small library and few

41

belongings on the back of his pet stag. He was no newcomer to Lough Ree for he had served his noviciate as a student under St. Diarmaid or Dermot on Inch Cleraun. It took him, it was said, three years and three months to establish the Hare Island monastery, of which only a few bare walls remain, before he moved south to Clonmacnois to become the patron saint of that famous theological college and burial place of kings.

Alas, though we were close to the protective walls of that great saint's church something of the diabolism of his Druid predecessors seemed to have entered our tent, for it leaked the whole night on my side only, the incessant dripping of water and the increasingly sodden state of my clothing making all but a few fitful snatches of sleep impossible.

Chapter 4

DOWN THE BARROW

E VEN in these latter days of diesel, a railway enthusiast who was invited to drive the *Flying Scotsman*, or the *Bristolian*, would welcome the idea as much as we did when we heard that John Williams required our help in taking a recently purchased barge down the Barrow River to Waterford, where he intended to use it for carrying agricultural machinery and livestock to and from Little Island, in the estuary of the River Suir.

We reached Dublin by noon the next day and were soon up at James Street harbour unloading our kit into the capacious hold of *M 71*, which looked in fine trim; a rectangle of welded steel plates 63 feet long, 13-foot beam, and powered by a Bolinder engine, she was able to carry up to 60 tons. The smoke-stack from the turf stove in the bow was sharpened to crown points which lent an Edwardian air of elegance, an attractively antique barrel contained her water supply and a metal tiller curved over the stern to control the large flat rudder which stood up out of the water. We could gather little about her history except that she was some thirty years old, had served mainly on the Barrow run and had been swept right over a weir above Carlow at a time when she was travelling light and the winter floods were exceptionally severe.

At James Street harbour we found that the nationalized transport concern which controls the inland waterways had recently sold all the cargo-carrying vessels and only a few remained as yet uncollected by their new owners, the last relics of a great fleet which had once sailed to the four corners of Ireland on a network which had served the country for over 120 years. This seemed to be the end of the canal transport era but since then pleasure boating has gone from strength to strength and, as Peter Denham wrote recently, "nobody would now dare to propose building a low bridge over the Shannon". There are hire cruiser bases at Killaloe, Portumna, Banagher, Shannon

Harbour, Athlone, Roosky, Jamestown, Carrick and Cootehall on the Shannon. On the Erne Navigation boats are at present available at Castle Archdale, Enniskillen and Belturbet. On the canal system they can be hired at Lucan, Carlow and Tullamore, and yet when, only a few years earlier, I wrote to try to obtain a boat, I was told that there were only two cruisers for hire on the entire inland waterway system.

So we sailed away into the setting sun as the Grand Canal turned westward, with many boatmen to help us on our way. They were eager to try their hands for the last time at the tiller and to offer invaluable advice on the foibles of aging engines. The waterway was already beginning to close in with a dense matting of weed encroaching on the clear centre from the rushy banks. I was instructed in the craft of the stopman by a bustling broad-shouldered fellow who confided to me that he had just consumed seven pints of stout and two glasses of whiskey, though this did not seem to have affected his dexterity. The stopman's job is to take a rope some 70 feet long which is attached to a metal retainer on the bow of the barge, and as the boat moves into the lock he has to wind it around a wooden bollard on the bank, tightening gradually so that the bow will be checked before it strikes the upper gates. When a crew is working fast the friction of the rope on the wood is so great that smoke may pour off it on a dry day, but we were working cautiously, for as one of the boatmen remarked, "The first shift's always the hardest!"

After moving up through a number of locks that evening we moored for the night well out in the country, and clambered down the ladder into the cabin at the bow. Betty Williams had cooked an excellent dinner on the *Shamrock* stove which gave the metal interior a glowing warmth and filled it with the pleasant, hazy scent of burning turf. I was reminded of an English couple who visited Ireland shortly after Hitler's war when petrol was still rationed and hired a car to tour the country, but discovered that they were strictly limited in fuel and so decided to see if they could obtain a little extra on the black market. Acting on the advice of their hotel porter they approached several vendors of newspapers at a variety of street corners until at last, when they were almost in despair they were slipped a bundle of coupons for a sum which remains undisclosed. The following day they set out to see Ireland, and when they stopped at a filling station they discovered that their illicit coupons entitled them to take away and burn to ashes something in the region of fifteen tons of good Irish turf.

As we worked the great barge on and up towards the summit level at Lowtown that day we gradually became more skilled at handling her, and so began to travel faster. We took a pride in trying to navigate the narrow bridges without scraping the hull on the stonework, and soon grew more dexterous at handling her in the locks. Late that night we reached Rathangan on the Barrow Branch of the Grand Canal where we were greeted warmly by Mr. Nolan who had been a private trader on the waterways for many years and greatly regretted the passing of the last working barges at a time when he would have been happy to continue to ply himself.

Away to the east we could see the low outline of the Wicklow Mountains where the River Liffey rises in a great reservoir. The same range conceals one of the most perfect settlements of the Celtic Church. I had seen Glendalough two years before and though it is not within immediate reach of the canal, would commend a visit to anyone passing that way by boat. Of the various saints associated with this wonderful monastery in the mountains, St. Coemgen, or Kevin is perhaps the most attractive because of his close association with wild animals. An otter kept his monastery supplied with a fresh salmon daily, and would bring it to the saint as he stood up to his waist in icy water reading his breviary.

Every Lent, Kevin would retire to a wattle hut on the side of the hill and stretch himself out in cross-vigil on the bare stone inside for a fortnight or even a month at a time, his only food being, as the chroniclers put it, "the music of the angels". One day a blackbird which had grown accustomed to Coemgen's company hopped down on to his outstretched hand, and after a brief inspection began to build her nest in the palm. So there the saint had to stay, almost motionless apart from an occasional sip of water, until all the little perishers had hatched out and flown away. Even when they had gone Coemgen continued his fast until an angel came along to put a stop to it.

"Come out of that hut," said the angel.

"I will not!" said the saint.

"Come out, or you'll die of starvation," said the angel.

"I'll not come out until I've obtained from God freedom from the judgement for myself and my monks, and maintenance of my churches within and without."

And these, wrote the chronicler, he obtained, and other benefits also, for it was held that those who made the pilgrimage to Glendalough seven times had made the equivalent of a pilgrimage to Rome.

The following day, scattered showers gave way to a powerful gale which slowed us down and showed us that there was more skill than we had fancied in keeping an unladen 60-ton barge free of banks, aqueducts and weed when the wind was catching her amidships. By the evening when we reached Athy we were thankful for the shelter of an overhanging loading shed at the edge of the town, for the tarpaulin covering *M 71*'s hold was far from watertight.

At Athy, Mick Hoare joined us as a pilot. The Barrow is a fast and tricky river and was then unbuoyed, and though Mick had not navigated it for some fourteen years, every inch of it was engraved on his memory. With such an expert pilot there were no problems attached to our journey down river, and we emerged at St. Mullins on the tidal estuary one bright, sunny afternoon, with a warm wind sweeping the clouds out of the sky.

St. Mullins was founded by St. Moling, a devout and ascetic man who was a disciple of St. Maedoc of Ferns in Wexford. One day as he was wading across a ford on the River Blackwater in the company of some worldly priests, he caught sight of St. Maedoc, and asked if he might join him to try his vocation. When the old saint died Moling was appointed Bishop of Ferns in his place, and moved his quarters to the episcopal hut. One of the older monks did his best to dissuade him:

"O Moling," he said, "no one has slept on that bed since St.

Maedoc died because of his great grace and holiness, for it was there that he would rest after his hard work and long prayers to God."

Moling was not to be dissuaded. "Whoever is bishop in his place," he said, "may fitly and rightly sleep in his bed."

No sooner had he stretched himself out than he was overcome by a dreadful cramp and an aching sickness. Had he lived at a later date he would doubtless have muttered to himself that it was all purely psychosomatic as he tossed and turned in agony. No amount of prayer availed him until at last he struck on the idea of calling on St. Maedoc to come to his rescue, whereupon the pains instantly vanished.

"It is true," he said ruefully, "that no man in the world in these days, however great his excellence and sanctity, is worthy to sleep or rest in the bed of Maedoc."

One day as he was sitting quietly meditating in the forest clearing at St. Mullins the saint saw a small wren pounce on a fly, but in a flash a cat jumped out and caught the wren. St. Moling instantly brought the wren back to life, and ordered it to show the same mercy to the fly.

And so we delivered *M 71* safely to her new anchorage in the estuary where she plied for a time carrying goods from Little Island to the mainland.

As we drove back across Ireland from Waterford to Lough Ree we were crossing a land which is subject to a gradual change of attitude and is emerging into an increasing maturity and tolerance. Anyone who is intrigued by sociology will know the terrible tale of Easter Island, where the inhabitants divided into two groups which warred against each other and ate their victims in remote caves. Though the civil wars and hatreds which divided the Irish for so long never reached such extremes of horror, blind racial, tribal and so-called religious influences still hold sway in some areas and among some sections of the community, though they are gradually waning.

At one extreme are those who still absurdly regard the Republicans as rebel colonists, while at the other end of the spectrum are those who look upon the British as being, without exception, rackrenting exploiters and evictors. Somewhere in a golden mean between the two lies the general opinion of a large majority of the younger generation of people whom one meets. The educational systems on both sides of the border are not without a measure of bias, but travelling abroad helps people to shed something of the insularity of their earlier outlook.

Inevitably industrialism is gradually increasing, though only slowly in a nation which is not blessed with considerable reserves of raw materials, though once, long ago, the gold of the Wicklow Mountains was exported in large quantities. The Republic is therefore mainly agricultural, though an increasing source of income is the growing tourist industry aided by a benevolent government which does its utmost to encourage the culinary art among a people never hitherto distinguished by any notable achievements in that quarter. Quite considerable progress has been made since the days when Irish cooking was divided stringently into three sections only, the fast, the feast and the "fry". The fast is more noted for the grace which accompanies it than for any gastronomic rewards. The "fry", which would appear at the strangest times of the day was really breakfast to which potatoes had been added as a kind of peace offering, and would always be accompanied by tea. The feast is really very good in its way, though somewhat overwhelming, and I find that I cannot compete with the following racy description of it by an author who cloaked himself under the title of *A Cosmopolite*, and made a sporting journey through Ireland about 1840:

"It is fair to do justice to the Irish in their feasts. They mean to be hospitable, and deem excessive profusion of edible matter the greatest proof of that intention. Unwilling, however, that you should lose that idea by any desultory succession, the whole is crammed on the table at once, without any regard to order or consistency; of wines, nothing is known. It is true, wine is placed on the table as a matter of form, to amuse the ladies, who, indeed, are the only people who do not treat it with negligence. But the instant the loads are removed from the table, a tumbler and wine glass, together with a small glass of hot water, are placed before each gentleman.

In the middle of the table are two glass flagons, each containing about a gallon of whiskey . . ."

No sooner have these been produced continues the *Cosmopolite*, than all the company "at once conceive that they have patriotism and sense, and are determined to prove that position!"

Chapter 5

A GLORY OF ISLANDS

THOSE who venture on to Lough Ree in a small boat are wise to keep an eye on wind and weather and we discussed it with Mr. and Mrs. Levinge who had invited us to spend an afternoon crossing the lake in the sturdy boat which Walter had built for his personal use. After tacking across the inner waters we sailed past Hare Island until we reached the open sea where the wind was raking up long uneven rollers with white crests and sending them bowling and racing across from the far shore. Walter pointed the bow straight into the waves and we huddled down in our oilskins as the whipped spray came flying over the boat. The sky was heavy with scurrying clouds but here and there the power of the wind had hacked a few blue windows among these grey battalions.

It was a welcome relief to be freed for a day from the rattling engine and uncertain wallowing of our own boat and to be voyaging in a craft superbly designed to cope with the steep, hurrying waves of the Shannon. We sailed close to the wind and the high gunwales of the yacht gave us that ample margin of safety from the choppy sea which was always sadly lacking on our own small craft.

On the offchance of catching fish we had dropped two lines with spinners on either side and just as we came abreast of Nun's Island and were rowing hard to avoid another tack we felt the sharp tug of a double catch – one got away as we were hauling it in but the other line produced an excellent perch of just over half a pound, and we ate him for breakfast the next morning. The clean feeding and fresh water of the lakes give these fish an excellent flavour akin to trout though they are more boney and generally smaller.

We sailed comfortably into the sheltered waters of St. John's Bay, and went ashore to explore the crumbling ivy-clad castle. Ireland is a land of castles, but few of them are in such a

50

magnificent setting as Rindoon, and fewer still were built on such a monumental scale. The peninsula juts out into the deep water of the lake providing the fortifications with a natural defence on three sides, while the fourth is protected by an artificial moat. Inland lie the shattered remnants of a long curtain wall which cuts off the entire neck of the peninsula and it was to this enclosure that the farmers would drive their cattle for sanctuary in time of trouble.

The earliest castle was a simple mote and bailey which is hidden among the trees, but this was superseded by the square keep of the Knights of St. John which, though ruined, still towers to a considerable height, and is so mantled in ivy that it is hardly possible to see the stonework at all. A bare outline in the turf marks the church of the Knights Hospitallers or Knights of St. John of Jerusalem, that veteran order which, with the Templars, called for swords about the cross and held at bay first the Saracens, and later the Turks. It was introduced into Ireland in 1183 and was divided into three sections, the military who fought mainly to protect the kingdom of Jerusalem and wore chain mail under a black robe and cowl, and a small white eight-pointed cross on the left breast; then there were the chaplains whose duties were mainly spiritual, and the serving brethren who were concerned with the maintenance of the other orders, and with the upkeep of the buildings and of the vast estates which provided sufficient income to keep this army of knights fed and accoutred. The order was governed by a council, over which ruled a Rector or Grand Master, a tried and hardy old campaigner who survived on the fringe of life, for many of the leaders of this little Christian army died in battle.

With the Moslem conquest of the Holy Land in 1291 the Hospitallers moved to Limasol, in Cyprus, and then in 1310 they conquered Rhodes where they remained until 1523. After a final stubborn siege they were driven westwards again, and found a natural fortress in Malta where they continued until the British captured the island from Napoleon. In 1879 the order moved to Rome, which has remained its headquarters, and it has been engaged in hospital work, so that the eight-pointed cross is familiar in most of the capitals of Christian countries, as a symbol of peace and healing where once it had heralded the glinting spears and square-hilted swords of a crusading army; a remarkable example of an institution which has adapted itself admirably to the changing demands of the different centuries since it first set out to aid the pilgrims who journeyed to the Holy Sepulchre.

As the long shadows creep across the ruined dungeons in the evening, the eye could well be deceived into seeing the cowled figure of a Knight Hospitaller under the ivy-clad walls, and other bleaker characters like Turgesius the Norseman who raided up the Shannon, and may well have fortified this point. He met his doom when he tried to marry the daughter of Malachy, King of Meath. Malachy ostensibly agreed to the match, but insisted on sending fourteen bridesmaids to accompany his daughter. The Norsemen were only too delighted and never dreamed that the damsels were really a picked band of carefully shaven fighting men. When the princess arrived and Turgesius was about to lead her out of the banqueting hall the Norsemen advanced on the 'maidens' who sank a dagger home into each one of them, and in the bloody fighting and confusion which followed Malachy stormed the fort and captured Turgesius whom he drowned gently and ceremoniously – probably in Lough Owel, just north of the Royal Canal at Mullingar.

In 968 the Norsemen were again raiding from fortified posts in this area when Brian, son of Kennedy, better known as Brian Boru raised a fleet and defeated them in a naval engagement on Lough Ree. He then strengthened this fort at Rindoon and reinforced it with a powerful garrison so that it was said that whoever held Rindoon held the key to Lough Ree. The outer wall was stormed and captured by Felim O'Conor in 1236, and he drove off all the cattle which had been gathered behind it for safety. Again, in 1270 both the wall and the castle were stormed and the keep burned by Hugh O'Conor of Connaught and Henry III fined the governor, James de Birmingham, 400 marks for failing to keep it safe.

So there can be few inches of this martial peninsula of Rindoon that have not been slippery with human blood at some time or other in its turbulent history, yet Harry Rice told us that he well remembered an old shepherd and his wife who lived there beneath the crumbling walls in a little cottage. "Now," he wrote, "they have passed on, and soon their tiny house will sink amongst the saplings and the weeds that fight for mastery upon the castle yard," and we agreed that this would not be one of the places in which we would choose to pass a night alone.

The wind was blowing half a gale when we provisioned the *Mary Ann* and set off to explore the remaining islands of Lough Ree and the Upper Shannon. We were looking forward to meeting more of the islanders but we regretted leaving the safe haven of Coosan. The long tricky swell of the open sea drove us inside Inchmore where we landed at a small pile of stones on the south-eastern shore. The Quigley family's cottage lies a little way inland, at the centre of a flat open space, and the sight of our strange oil-skinned figures alarmed the younger children, who gave us one look of wild surmise, darted into the house, and left the dog barking courageously from the protective covering of the doorway. Even the chickens seemed distressed by our sudden appearance, but Mrs. Quigley came out to welcome us and offer us a seat by the glowing fire.

Inchmore, or Great Island, is the largest on Lough Ree, and we were surprised to learn that there was only one other person, apart from the Quigley family, still living on it. Mrs. Quigley seemed very happy there, though often alone when her husband was away fishing, and all she seemed to fear was the prospect of being cut off from supplies by stormy weather during the winter; though this had not happened during the last four years, shortly before then the island had been completely isolated from the mainland, less than a mile away, for six full weeks, and its inhabitants unable to purchase supplies for most of that time. I asked what happened if the children were ill, but the lack of visitors preserves them from contagious diseases, and as they looked so healthy it was hard to imagine that they ever suffered from more than the mildest ailments.

We thought that Inchmore had the most delightful

atmosphere of all the larger islands on Lough Ree. It is of a sufficient size to have good roads which wind down through the half-neglected fields. There is now so little traffic that these have grown green, and the uncut hedges have sprung up high, fending off the lake winds and sheltering these lanes into traps for the sun.

It was a longish walk to Jim Tiernan's place and when we knocked on the door of his two-storied house he imagined that we must have been shipwrecked. No doubt we must often in our voyage have looked as though we had come from under rather than over the water, but Jim explained his concern by saying that his last visitors a few weeks before had been a dinghy-load of ladies from a cabin cruiser which had run aground on one of the several tricky shoals in Portlick Bay. Fortunately there had been little danger as the lake was in one of its gentler moods at the time, but their experience had been sufficiently unpleasant to prove that these waters cannot be navigated without the essential charts printed by the Athlone Press.

Jim Tiernan was in his seventies; a man of powerful build with a broad weatherbeaten face and penetrating eyes which looked through one disconcertingly. Having grown up before education was made obligatory for the islanders he neither reads nor writes, though he can perceive in sky and water much that is a closed book to the city-dweller. He owned some forty acres on Inchmore, and was also the proprietor of the ghostly, bird-haunted Nun's Island away to the west. When we had pitched our tent by the old grass-grown quay I asked him what he thought of the Lough Ree monster, and was surprised when he leaned towards me and said:

"I've seen it as close as you're standing now! Looming up out of the mist!"

Though startled by this sudden admission of the improbable, I was fortunate enough to notice a faint twinkle in his eye.

"It moved towards me, growing larger and larger . . ." He paused dramatically, "and then suddenly it turned into an otter with her young trailin' behind her! But who knows? I may have been deluded by all that I saw."

A GLORY OF ISLANDS

It would be absurd to argue with either Walter Levinge or
Jim Tiernan about whatever is, or is not to be found beneath
the peaty waters of Ree, or indeed of some fifty or sixty other
lakes in the west of Ireland, but there still remained the mysterious white cow. Was it empirical or mythological? Here and
there I caught a rumour of it from those who lived on or near
to the lakes, and though I never met a soul who had actually
seen it himself, none would jest about it as Jim had jested about
the monster. With the white cow it was always a more serious
matter, with a "Me feyther saw it," or "I had an uncle now, did
ye ever hear of him . . ." or "I knew a feller once . . ."

As we talked on with this old master of the waters time
seemed to stand still in a way that it does not do on the mainland. The evening gathered in a little with a few late bees tumbling out of the clover, but there were no clocks to whirr and
chime and peace seemed to have gathered itself and settled
around us. As we learned more of the lives of these lake-
dwellers I began to realize the real reason why the islands are
being so rapidly depopulated. It is not that these people are
made of less stern material than their forefathers, or are much
more attracted by the tinsel values of the city, though this may
draw away a few; the real reason is that the law requires them
to educate their children, and to do so they must have a school-
teacher. Within living memory, indeed within the last fifty years,
there were ninety-two men, women and children living on Inchmore and its neighbouring island of Inchturk (they were then
connected by a causeway which was a great source of conten-
tion, but the winter gales have removed most of it). Now there
is only Jim Tiernan and the Quigleys, and when Jim has gone
and the Quigley children have to be educated there may be no
one left on an island which has been inhabited for at least three
thousand years. The islanders are, I was told by an authority on
the lakes, almost certainly of the original Iberian stock which inhabited Ireland before the Celts came. It would be a sorry
business if they had to go for ever, leaving these rich pastures to
occasional farming from the mainland, to the care of the
carrion crows, plaintive curlews and voracious brambles and
ivy which have already swallowed all but the largest of their

55

buildings. The Nolan family had gone out on to the mainland quite recently and the Quigleys will probably follow them, for if the children are not sent to school a fine is imposed until the family is willing to comply with the regulations.

You may then witness here the end of a very ancient, sturdy and independent people. Education is compulsory in Ireland. No schoolmaster can be persuaded to stay indefinitely and schoolmistresses are apt to marry rapidly in this environment. After all the passing centuries a tradition of life is being obliterated by a just law which is intended to benefit the lake-fishermen, but is certainly not for the benefit of the islands which they once cultivated, for the hay in some of those excellent fields had not been cut for several years. It is true that the islands were once overcrowded. On Inchturk there was a man who raised a family of fourteen children on half an acre of land, though his meagre tillage was supplemented by the money which he made from fishing. That they grew up remarkably fit and healthy remains a tribute to fish as a diet, and to the excellence of the island climate.

We learned much about fishing from Jim Tiernan; of the hard nights setting the eel-lines in the summer – long lines marked at either end by a float tied to a sunken rock. The float may be set miles out into the heart of the lake, but the islanders can return unerringly to the right spot to collect it again. We learned of the great rollers 20 feet high, between which, as Jim put it, "It is, for a moment, so still you can light your pipe, for the wall of water shuts out the wind altogether." We learned of the long, harsh work netting for pike on winter nights when the wind seems to dissect the flesh from the bone like a surgeon's knife, and the water is filled with sharp edges of ice like shattered panes of glass. Even on such nights as this the men will sleep away from home, curling under a calico sail supported on light and pliable willow twigs, and this will keep them completely dry as long as they do not touch the cotton cloth on the inside.

All down the centuries the islanders have been struggling to assert their independence against authority and on Ree there was a sufficient number of them to enable them to win out for a time. If their general antagonist is any brand of authority, their specific one is the water bailiff. The task of these bailiffs has been to ensure that the lakes are not over-fished and to maintain plenty of stock, and especially trout. The islanders feel that their livelihood is at stake and that the lake has been their private preserve since time immemorial : that they have the right to fish wherever and whenever they please, as their ancestors did before them.

The islanders keep their own fish ponds, well stocked with trout, and these the bailiffs decided to fill in. Some years ago they came out to Inchmore with a posse of police and started to bring the largest stones they could find and heave them in, but no sooner had a bailiff dropped his than an islander would wade in and take it out again, and after a while the law gave up the unequal struggle. The next attack was when they tried to prevent the islanders from netting for fish. Boatloads of police and bailiffs were concealed early one morning just outside Coosan Point where they ambushed a party which had been netting in the inner lakes. They managed to get some of them to court but the islanders are still netting their fish.

Quite recently the islanders were summonsed for selling trout before the beginning of the fishing season, and were brought before the magistrate on the morning the season opened although the offence had been committed earlier.

"When did you catch these fish?" asked the magistrate.

"Sure, your Honour, they were caught last season and we've been holding them in the fishpond ever since," came the reply. The case was dismissed.

The authorities remained anxious to improve the standard and quantity of trout available and raise the tourist potential of this area so they sought to buy the islanders out of fishing with nets by offering a lump sum of compensation, but the claims which were put forward ran far too high.

Only those who knew it well appreciated the comparative simplicity of the island life until recent years. While England employs a maze of gadgets these people have no electricity and little time for machinery. They use boats instead of cars and though a few hang outboard motors over the stern, Jim Tiernan told us that he thought nothing of rowing seven miles across the lake to Athlone and back again the same evening. Quite recently one was invited aboard a visiting yacht and offered tinned peaches, which he turned down with a mild look of revulsion. He imagined that they must be raw eggs, and it was only later when he was persuaded to try them against his better judgement, that he liked them so much that he bought an entire crate and ate little else for several days.

Money has been another disintegrating factor in the island life. During Hitler's war, when food was scarce, eels and fish reached an unprecedented premium, and for the first time the islanders had an exceptional amount of spare cash to play with. Some of them devoted their new-found wealth to putting themselves in touch with the hitherto largely mysterious world which lay beyond their natural hunting and fishing grounds in the lake district. For several generations they had known of the outside world by hearsay from children or relations who had emigrated, but few of those who remained could find the opportunity to travel far.

About 1942 one party of men set off to visit Dublin for the first time, and met with a variety of mishaps. They booked into a comfortable hotel, and after a pleasant evening in the bar decided to turn in and went up to their bedroom. The electric light, which had been left on for them presented a grave puzzle; they were accustomed to oil lamps, and had no idea how to turn it off. Eventually after a good deal of discussion, one of them solved the problem dramatically by taking off his boot and aiming a good hard swipe at the bulb. It is said that they were surprised and impressed by the simplicity of the switch arrangement when it was demonstrated to them in the morning.

Another who paid a visit to the lavatory imagined that the sudden inrush of water would inevitably flood the entire hotel, so he tried to stop it with his foot, praying the while to St. Diarmaid, who was occasionally given to walking on the water when in his more ascetic moods, and behold, the flood ceased, almost immediately. With that rare Irish gift of genuine humour, the islanders will tell such tales even against themselves, but before we smile at them we could ask ourselves how many of us could trim the wick or clean the glass funnel of an oil lamp when the smoke had blackened it, or indeed how long we could survive alone on Nun's Island with nothing but a little fishing tackle.

The deserted schoolhouse, a solidly-built and well-roofed place, lay just beyond Tiernan's house, and over the door was an inscription in Gaelic. The first school on Inchmore was put up about 1900, but the islanders, realizing that this was a far greater threat to their independence than a regiment of water bailiffs, promptly burned it to the ground. The present building has a certain charm; just one room with a fireplace at the end, a storeroom, and an impressive porch to keep the cold lake winds from the unopened front door in winter. The desks were piled high against the wall, only slightly marked with those incisions with which children love to while away the duller hours. A window-pane had been broken and a bird had nested in the open cupboard where once the notebooks and pencils had reposed in stately order. The hearth was piled high with sticks and twigs where the remains of twenty years of birds nests had cascaded down the chimney. Oliver Goldsmith lived only a few miles east of this little school, and painted his timeless portrait of its typical master:

> *I knew him well, and every truant knew:*
> *Well had the boding tremblers learned to trace*
> *The day's disasters in his morning face;*
> *Full well they laughed with counterfeited glee*
> *At all his jokes, and many a joke had he;*
> *Full well the busy whisper circling round*
> *Conveyed the dismal tidings when he frowned.*
> *Yet he was kind, or, if severe in aught,*
> *The love he bore to learning was in fault . . .*

When we had made our camp on the old quay beyond the empty schoolhouse we set out to explore the rest of Inchmore. A road, which is gradually closing in, leads up from the quay to what was once the great house near the highest point of the island. The building is matted with ivy, but some of the stones are so old that they must have come from the Celtic monastery on the north shore, of which there is little left standing above the wind-mown turf. The kitchen garden of the old house was one of the most impressive that I had seen, with walls of solid stone rising over 20 feet high. Behind this abandoned ruin itself were several dilapidated cottages serving as memorials to those who once tilled and cultivated the fields around. Jim Tiernan had told us that the big house was once a fortified outpost of the Dillon family which held Portlick Castle across the bay; later it had passed to various families with English names, and that the Tiernans were kinsmen of the Dillons. On the eastern side of the island, which takes the full brunt of the prevailing wind and is not inhabited, we found that an oak forest was gradually creeping out across the fields, and by coincidence I was thinking of that strange apparition, the white creature of Inchbofin, part myth and part reality, about which the islanders had told me so much, when suddenly a luminous white face with two burning eyes emerged from the top of the hedge a few inches above my face. Following so swiftly on my train of thought, it took me a moment to realize that it was a perfectly ordinary head of a white cow, which snorted and vanished.

As we sat by the lake's edge on the grass-covered quay the last embers of that wonderful, windy day on Inchmore burnt themselves out, the ripple of lake water provided a background of gentle music, and a vast full moon hoisted itself gradually over the rim of the sea. As it rose from the horizon it seemed to build a path of silver from the land's end right across the glittering surface of the lake, so firm and yet so delicate that we felt as though we could walk across it into the enchanted world of Irish folklore where there is neither good nor evil, but only a price to be paid by those mortals who are foolish enough to return to the land from which they came.

The next morning as we crossed the bay to Portlick Castle, we suddenly noticed, as we looked down at the rocks, that the reflected sunlight shining through the clear lake water near the shore, had turned all beneath it into a deep rich gold. It seemed as though the *Mary Ann* was floating over a vast store of treasure where whole rocks and crags and promontories had been transmuted by the touch of some forgotten Irish Midas.

We were travelling at three or four knots and peering rather dreamily down at this vision of untold wealth which reminded me of the legends of the magic skill of the Welsh heroes at turning fungus into gold, though the spell, it was said, lasted only a day or two before the substance melted into a black and stinking hash. From these remote speculations we were removed by a sudden and vicious jerk. There followed a resounding crack as the bow struck the reef but we continued to move forward and the entire boat was levered some six inches higher in the water, while from down under came the sinister crackling rumble of metal and wood grating over solid rock. The engine juddered and raced frantically before expiring in an extra puff of blue smoke while the propeller gave a few final convulsions. The boat continued to grind forward and then dropped gently and peacefully into deeper water beyond the reef. We had committed the cardinal sin of failing to keep our customary watch on the chart, but the *Mary Ann*, though she leaked considerably more after this experience, still kept going; indeed, I fancy that her tough old timbers suffered rather less than our nerves, for it is a disturbing experience to be travelling in a boat at one level and to be suddenly and briefly elevated to a higher plane. We limped to a mooring just below Portlick Castle which we had been invited to visit, and from the battlements we could see many of the islands spread out around the lake beneath us like an ancient perspective map until they blended and vanished into the horizon.

Just as Rindoon dominates the north and the west of Lough Ree, so Portlick commands the southern and eastern approaches. The tall hump of an old mote and bailey castle lies a little to the south-east, and is almost identical with one at St. Mullins, on the Barrow Navigation. These wooden forts had a small keep, and a large enclosure for protecting cattle in times of trouble, for the main sport of the Irish down the centuries was raiding each others herds – a habit which they were later to export with their emigrants to the west of America.

Portlick Castle was built in the sixteenth century, and is a rectangular tower house of a kind common all over the country. There is a small door with a space above for shooting down at besiegers; inside is a trap-door in the roof for stabbing down at

61

unwelcome guests and known as a "murdering-hole", while the narrow spiral staircase winds to the right so that any assailant would be at the disadvantage of having to use his spear or his sword in his left hand. The steps of the stair were at differing heights to trip the enemy as they fought their way up, and these must have caused some ripe Irish oaths from the Dillons' more bibulous guests and distant relations, as they ricocheted spirally downwards after one of those old-fashioned Irish feasts.

Over towards Ladywell, another large house to the east, we found the local cemetery, gathered around the remains of a church which was in ruins. We dug a little into the warm black loam to uncover the proud record of one of the departed Dillons who had married a daughter of the King of Meath, thus binding this invading Plantagenet family to one of the ancient loyalties of the country in an astutely political bond of blood.

After Portlick we moved north, past Leveret Island into Saints Bay, where a long rolling swell from the west wind carried us swiftly to the mouth of the River Inny. A new land drainage scheme was opening the marshlands to the east by deepening the bed of this river, but it had not yet scooped out the mouth, and though our engine battled hard against the fast-flowing current, after less than half a mile we came to two sharp bends, where we ran aground. As soon as we tried to get free the water picked our little boat up like driftwood and flung her against the bank, nearly tipping us both out, and there we drifted for a few unpleasant moments until the engine picked up again, and the current spat us back into the lake at a great speed, as though the Inny was determined to expel all who might infringe or invade its fastnesses. As a lock-keeper once remarked, the *Mary Ann* "will go almost anywhere it's wet", but the Inny defeated her.

The countryside around this river is flat, with the tall Shannon reeds obscuring most of the delta. The wind went whistling through them, bending them like a wave in the corn, but the great rollers from the lake died quickly among their closely mustered roots. Sheldrake and mallard rose wheeling and crying round the boat, and an old farmhouse leaned gauntly against the sky – occasionally a brief shower would break across the lake, blinding out our view, and then vanish almost as soon as it had come. We snatched a hasty meal in the cabin and turned the bow of our old boat towards the narrow and tricky gap between Inchbofin and the mainland. On the map this looks easy enough to navigate, but on the charts it becomes a slender thread between the jagged teeth of uneven ranges of rocks and shoals. We bobbed very cautiously past the tip of the island in a bumpy sea, and breathed more freely as we chugged out into the deeper water beyond.

At Mayne's Lodge we found an excellent stone harbour which must be approached with caution owing to silting near the entrance, and there we moored to look at the delightful artificial lake. Then we drove the *Mary Ann* back towards Inchmore with the west wind piling the breakers against her hull on the starboard side until she rolled over to the gunwales and we had to turn and run before the waves for a while.

Back on the quay at Inchmore Jim Tiernan came down to ask us how we had fared, and whether there was any way in which he could help us. We offered him an aluminium camp chair which he approached with some caution, picked up with his little finger, and remarked wonderingly, "The Devil, but it's got the lightness in it!" When we offered him a drink he raised his glass of stout to Kay and said :

"Here's to the porter, and wishing it was wine,
And here's to my old heart, and wishing I had thine!"

We talked on into the cool of the evening until the stars grew out of the paleness of the twilight and the moon rose among thin slivers of cloud which might have been combed shorewards across the sky with a hay-rake. In the west the evening shaded away through infinite gradations of pale blue and turquoise and the dew could be heard as it formed on the grass. At length Jim came back to his favourite subject of fishing saying that the greatest pike that he had ever handled had, it was true, got away. He was an old man when he hooked it, and it was as long as the boat he was in, and very broad : a vast monster like a shark. He fought it for hours, and his description reminded me of Hemingway's old man alone in battle with the creatures of the deep. Eventually he got the monster alongside, but as he reached forward to the kill it snapped his line with its final bid for life and vanished in a great rush of water which would have capsized a less experienced fisherman.

Then he told us of the time he had been up in St. John's Bay when he saw a man shouting and waving for help. Rowing over he found him struggling with a vast pike, and out of its mouth was sticking the foot of a young calf. Taking out his knife he slit open the pike's gullet and extracted the calf carefully from the fish's maw, for it was still alive. There he paused dramatically before he completed his tale: "And sure," he said, "and that calf, it grew up and lived to a ripe ould age!"

1
Islands
on Lough Corrib

2a Mr Harry Johnston (right) of Little Paris Island.

2b Bow-hauling the *Mary Ann* up the Barrow Navigation.

Chapter 6

SACRED PIG ISLAND

As we left the comforting shelter of the quay at Inchmore the wind gathered its forces from the south and came over and past us with a steady roar, so that when we emerged into the open sea vast rollers gathered under the stem of the boat and lifted us until we seemed to be surf-riding high on the lake. The boat rose and fell some 20 feet or more on these surging rollers and we could understand what Jim Tiernan meant by the almost uncanny stillness which reigns in the trough between each wave, for the grey walls of moving water tower above your head and cut the wind off altogether. Luckily they were not breaking on the crests for that could have tipped us over but the gale was rising and whipping spray off the top of them so that we glanced over our shoulders apprehensively. A thin rain from an overcast sky kept us huddled in our oilskins and it seemed as though the ancient gods of these waters were anxious to expel the foreigners who had so long presumed to pry into a few of their secrets.

When these long rollers had flung us swiftly up the length of the waterway we sighted the buoy on the Iskeraulin shoal, opposite the entrance to the short Lecarrow Canal which was built for carrying stone from inland quarries. This canal runs up to the village, about a mile to the west, and has been dredged and cleared by an enlightened government as a safe haven for small craft sailing this frequently stormy corner of the lake.

We landed on the south east of Inch Cleraun or Quaker Island as it used to be called after a Mr. Fairbrother who built himself a house and was living there in 1837. Unfortunately this good man had, like so many people of that period, very scant respect for ancient monuments, and began to tear down and cart away for his own use quantities of stone from the churches of the noble Celtic monastery nearby. But he had not reckoned with the patron of the place, St. Diarmaid or Dermot, who smote the poor carthorse with the bolt of his holy vengeance. Not only

E   65

did the beast go mad and career all round the island so danger-
ously that it had to be shot with a musket, but every living
creature from the cows and sheep to the dog and cat followed
suit, and it was said that even the bumble-bees were flying
upside-down and looping the loop until eventually the Quaker
gave in and resolved not to take any more of the stone, whereupon peace and normality reigned once again in his island
kingdom.

On Inch Cleraun we found the same sad tale of depopulation,
but here there was an added reason. The Farrell's house was
just above the landing-stage, but the roof had fallen in on one
side. I had been told that the family had 'gone out' of the
island, as they say in these parts, because of a curious manifestation in the form of a penetrating coldness which would fill
the living-room, generally at a time when the man of the house
was away fishing. Even on a warm summer night it would grow
so cold that you could put your hand on the glass of the oil-
lamp and notice no heat at all – a statement which is startling
enough to those of us who have scorched our fingers in that way.
It seemed that this icy atmosphere issued from a point just
above the window, and indeed I did feel a certain sensation of
coldness and unease when I sat in the room. Soon the last trusses
of the roof will have crumbled altogether and perhaps the
strange atmosphere of the place will be carried on the night wind
away across the turbulent waters of Lough Ree.

We met Paddy Walsh in the rain as we crossed the side of the
hill. A tall, broad-shouldered man, he owns most of the island –
perhaps 180 acres or more of some of the finest grazing in those
parts. Now that the Farrells have gone he is a complete hermit,
and courageous enough to live a mile from the shore in the
roughest part of the lake – particularly in the hard winters when
the icebergs which form in this area can cut off all communica-
ton for long stretches at a time. But when he spoke his voice was
deep and confident. No, he said that he had never seen the
Lough Ree monster, but there were more things in the lake than
were understood. "My father saw a white cow and a calf come
up from under the lake and on to Inchmore, and they galloped
around the fields and then they went back into the waters again,

by the light of the moon," he said, "and he saw that as certainly as I stand here!"

"That's very strange," I said, finding it difficult to conceal my surprise.

"Ah, and what's strange about it," said Mr Walsh, in his deep booming voice. "There's plenty of things in this world that we don't understand, and plenty of things in the lake, too! Those three priests who saw something were good men, and there are things, certainly there are things in that lake that we don't understand."

Mr. Walsh shook his head at the mystery of it all, and the thin rain poured down around us, running off our oilskins, but soaking deep into his clothes, though this seemed to worry him not at all, and he took us along to see the island.

Only a little way from where we stood was a green hollow sweeping down to the angry water where once, so the legends relate, that redoubtable matriarch Queen Maeve built herself a summer palace. Maeve or Medb seems to have combined the martial gifts of Boadicea with the marriage ethics of Mary Queen of Scots, for when she was not fighting she was marrying, and when she was not marrying she was generally at war. Her first husband was Conor, King of Ulster, but after a fateful series of disagreements with him she rode out in a fury posthaste for the court of her father Eochaid who was reputedly King of Meath about 100 B.C. Maeve remained awhile at Tara, and if indeed her character is based on historical reality Medb's mound there may well have been her temporary home.

Next, to improve diplomatic relations with the neighbouring kingdom of Connaught, Eochaid of Tara decided to remarry Maeve to King Ailill in the hope that she would have better luck the second time, but not long afterwards Ailill died, leaving his termagant wife as the undisputed queen of the mountainous and warlike west. It was at this point that Maeve began her long series of battles with the men of Ulster which made her perhaps the most outstanding character in any of the great religious sagas of the Irish Druids, and the source of some of the noblest Irish folklore called the *Tain Bo Chuailgne* or Raiding of the Cattle of Cooley. Maeve came close to conquering Ulster in her wars but that nation had bred a remarkable hero. The Queen was forewarned of this champion by a wise woman before she took up arms; the Druidess was asked to prophesy victory but instead kept crying of blood that was crimson and blood that was red, and that on the troops of the Connaught army :

I see a small man doing deeds of arms, though there are many wounds on his smooth skin; the light of the heroes shines like the rays of the sun about his head, and there is victory on his brow. Young and beautiful is he, and modest; richly-clothed, and yet he slays like a dragon in battle. His arms and his valour are the mark of Cuchulain of Muirthemne.

Maeve was still eager to go to war for she longed to avenge herself on her former husband, Conchobar or Conor, the King of Ulster and by her charms and spells she had won over Fergus MacRoy, the former champion of the North to her own side. By the same methods but with even stronger magic she sought to seduce Cuchulain from his allegiance in a clandestine meeting, but she got short shrift from him and all she could obtain was an agreement that the champion would engage one of her own picked swordsmen every day in single combat as long as her invading army halted until dawn as soon as the duel was over.

In battle after battle Cuchulain was victorious until he was so covered with wounds that not a pin could be put between them and his clothes had to be kept from touching his body by a wickerwork of willow twigs stuffed with hay. Maeve even sent out to challenge him the wizard Calatin who could turn himself into seventy warriors, but with the aid of another Cuchulain slew them all one by one.

Eventually Conor and the men of Ulster roused themselves from the apathy caused by the magic of Druids and came to the aid of Cuchulain and the heroes who had held the frontier, and there was peace for a time. So far the wonderful old tale has perhaps some of its roots in history, but at this point it departs into the realm of total myth with a tale of how Cuchulain went down to the mysterious island of the Celtic Other World or Dun Scaith, and though assailed by serpents and gigantic toads, he and his companions carried off the gold and silver of Hell, three head of magic cattle, and a mystical cauldron which provided an inexhaustible supply of food.

Meanwhile Maeve had married herself another husband. The youngest son of the King of Leinster, his name was also Ailill, much to the confusion of the unfortunate Irish historians who have a sufficient number of problems trying to distinguish fact from fiction, let alone one Ailill from the other. Though they bickered a good deal, this was a marriage of love rather than of political expediency, and lasted until Ailill was slain in battle by Conall Cernach, a blood-letting which encouraged the Leinstermen to invade the North.

Cuchulain went out to war again, but Maeve had woven an alliance of the South which included armies from Munster, Leinster, Connaught and Meath which came raiding the cattle and burning and destroying. After killing three enemy Druids with his harpoon throwing spears, Cuchulain was run through by Lugaid, son of that King of Munster whom the northern hero had killed years ago for the sake of a woman over whom they had quarrelled.

Cuchulain crawled to the nearest lake where he drank deeply and then, leaving a trail of blood behind he was carried by his enemies to a pillar-stone to which he strapped himself with a belt so that he should die facing his foes with his weapons in his hands. Those who had conquered him drew off to a respectful distance and as though to fulfil his destiny, down from the sky came Morrigu the hooded crow and goddess of war to perch on his shoulder, the light of the heroes which had always shone around his head in battle faded as his life blood flowed from him, but his war-horse, the Gray of Macha came back to fight for him, and killed many of the enemy with his teeth and hoofs.

So fell one of the noblest heroes of ancient Ireland, but Maeve mourned the death of Ailill her husband and came to build her summer palace where we stood on Inch Cleraun, among the tall groves of the Druid university founded there by her sister Clorina, from whom the island takes its name.

It was natural that Maeve should make her retreat among the Druids who had woven such mighty spells to aid her invasions and had themselves fought time and again with sword and with propaganda against the men of Ulster. Though she had the morals of a film-star, the Queen had retained an ageless beauty, and on warm days she would slip off her clothes and slide naked into the cool waters of a pool by the lake's edge, or lie sunbathing among the loosestrife and meadowsweet on the green hillside.

Now Forbaid, a son of that King Conor of Ulster by another wife was determined to avenge his country's wrong, and after spying out the little green hollow in which we stood, and practising hour after hour with his sling until it was said that he could hit an apple at a remarkable distance, he rode south of the border and lay in ambush until the ageing queen, her guards all keeping at a respectful distance, came down to bathe in her pool. With a quick fling of his arm Forbaid shot his stone with deadly accuracy so that it sank through his victim's temple and killed her outright; before the hue and cry began he was away and riding like one possessed for his own land.

So died the fighting Queen of Connaught, and by an act which was definitely against the local equivalent to the MCC rules for cattle raiding, for even though Maeve herself had not always played the war game strictly according to the standard moral code, she had at least generally paid a lip-service to it. The men of Connaught came and carried her body away to Sligo to what is now called the Yeats Country, and all the nation and armies came to fling their stones on the cairn over her body on top of the mountain called Knocknarea until they raised one of the vastest sepulchral monuments in these islands, for the circumference at the base is 630 feet, the slope to the crown 80 feet, and the diameter on top about 100 feet. The whole cairn is made up of quite small stones piled in such staggering profusion that one is reminded of primeval monuments like the pyramids or the Aztec sacrificial mounds. Around it the great grey lichened boulders bulge from the ground as though a crock of gold was buried beneath each one of them.

In time Maeve found her place in mythology as Mab, the queen of the fairies and joined the hosting of the sidhe (pronounced shee) whose winged horses speed through the middle air, hunting and possibly doing a little cattle raiding on the side, and in Yeats' great poem, "The Hosting of the Sidhe":

> *The host is riding from Knocknarea*
> *And over the grave of Clooth-na-bare . . .*
> *Our arms are waving, our lips are apart;*
> *And if any gaze on our rushing band,*
> *We come between him and the deed of his hand,*
> *We come between him and the hope of his heart.*

When you stand on the crown of that tall cromlech and the wind is coming up from the Atlantic past Sligo and tearing grey shreds of mist like shrouded Druids past you, it does not take a great deal to conjure up:

> *. . . that sliding silver-shoed,*
> *Pale silver-proud queen-woman of the sky . . .*

who has woven her potent spells and leased her enchantments to the poetry and literature of all the kingdoms of Britain.

Most of the finest tales of the hero Cuchulain and of the loves and wars of Queen Maeve have been preserved for posterity only by remarkable good fortune. *The Book of the Dun Cow* was rewritten by a monk called Maelmuiri who was murdered by robbers at Clonmacnois Abbey in the year 1106. Earlier this same scribe had been a member of the community on Friar's Island, which is now virtually a peninsula jutting out into the inner lakes to the west of Coosan. We had walked out to the monastery, which lies on the eastern shore of the island, and had found a fairly large church and the jumbled foundations of many other buildings in a dense wood close to a point where the ground slopes steeply down to the entrance to Ballykeeran Lough. Certainly this should be a place of reverence and pilgrimage to all Irish scholars, for it was there that Maelmuiri copied the most important store of ancient Gaelic mythology, and gave it the delightful title of *The Book of the Dun Cow* because the tattered and faded original manuscript was either written on or bound in parchment which had once been the hide of St. Ciaran's favourite cow, which was dun-coloured – the deepish red of modern Sussex cattle. The first book must

71

therefore have been written about the close of the seventh century but unfortunately only a fragment of 138 pages of the copy remains intact, and this is in the library of the Royal Irish Academy.

A few hundred yards from the scene of the murder of Queen Maeve is the great monastery and former university, or perhaps one should call it a theological college, which was founded by St. Diarmaid or Dermot, who was a descendant of the last pagan King of Meath. He probably landed on the island in the early sixth century, and to the Druids who met him on the shore he declared that he came in peace to tell them of grace and of the saving of mankind. Inch Cleraun was a more than ordinarily fascinating island monastery: there had already been a major Druidic religious centre there, and the Christian settlement which followed it was to adapt many of the best of the Druid customs while at the same time abolishing those which were repellant to the faith. And so the burning of sacrificial offerings of men, women and children gradually ceased, but the extreme asceticism was retained. The mixing of poisonous potions and the muttering of incantations was severely condemned, but the hermit sought his own salvation much as the individual Druid had done, and the complicated discipline of modern monasticism would have been entirely foreign to the system. In the place of the Ollamh, or chief Druid stood the abbot, but the gaily-coloured and gracefully draped mantles worn by the senior Druids and made from the skin and feathers of innumerable birds gave way to the sober hood and dark robes of the servants of the Nazarene, with its emphasis on poverty and the abnegation of the hollow delights of this brief and transitory life in the certainty of a deeper spiritual reward. The abler Druids were servants of the state: masters of political expediency, and often warriors in their own right, they sat at Queen Maeve's right hand and were almost philosopher kings, but initially the Celtic Church set out to bring a simple message of love and peace and charity rather than to meddle about in politics – an ideal which it was not long able to sustain.

While most of the buildings of the monastery would have been of wood, the six remaining churches are built of solid stone joined together, Mr Walsh told us, by a cement which was mixed with the blood of oxen to give it an immensely hard consistency. The wooden halls, though they have vanished, have left curious mounds here and there in the turf, showing that domestic buildings once covered a considerable area.

The largest church is the ruined Clogas, or bell tower which stands near the centre of the highest point on the island, and is traditionally the site of the first oratory of St. Diarmaid himself. The bell tower is not the usual round building capped by a stone cone, but is square like a parish church, and was described with a glint of Irishness by Harry Rice as the only square round tower in the country. It was probably built about the tenth century, but the main body of the church is a good deal earlier and an arch of the eastern window is scooped out of a single rock. On the north wall is a stone with a hole bored through to the outside which is a feature of several of the churches on Lough Ree. It may have been used to dispose of the consecrated host quickly to the faithful, so that it would not be desecrated by raiding warriors in time of trouble, or it may have served to pass the host to women or to lepers who were not always allowed to mingle with the congregation.

No doubt the Clogas Church was built for the use of the laity – a parish church for the people of Inch Cleraun and for the growing number of Christians on the mainland and neighbouring islands. The main monastery was gathered nearer the lake within a vast stone-walled enclosure which must be nearly a mile in circumference, though only parts of it now show above the turf. The largest church there is called Teampul Mor – the Great Church, which measures $47\frac{1}{2}$ feet from east to west, and 21 feet from north to south. On the left of the altar is a doorway leading into a small room which may have been used as a penitentiary or hermit's cell, or as a vestry, and indeed may have served all three purposes at various times. There are some signs of a cloister garth by the walls of this church which suggest that it was later used by Cistercians or Dominicans who came to Ireland about 1250, at the invitation of Maurice Fitzgerald.

Teampul Diarmaid, which is said to have been built by the founder saint, lies a little to the south. Measuring only 8 feet by

7 feet wide, this can lay good claim to being the smallest church in the land, for by definition a church must be large enough to hold the essential two or three who are gathered together, and anything smaller would be a cell rather than a church. The steep gable, which probably once supported a stone slab roof, the side walls which are prolonged to serve as buttresses and the little doorway with its lintel of a single piece of stone all support the theory that this oratory was constructed about the year 524, when Ciaran, then a boy of twelve years old, came to study the trade of sanctity under his tutor, St. Diarmaid.

The Chancel Church, and the little Church of the Dead were too overgrown with nettles and briars at the time of our visit to enable us to give them more than a cursory glance but the Women's Church, which lies to the south in a separate walled enclosure, is of particular interest. In the earliest monasteries like Inch Cleraun the monks and nuns were not segregated into different communities miles apart, but trusting to the high standard of morality which grew out of an even higher standard of asceticism, they lived at first in the same enclosure, and the men coped mainly with the agriculture, cattle and fishing, while the women concentrated on the cooking, maintenance and clothing. The Women's Church is a fascinating example of the first stage in the disintegration of this early Christian ideal; it is set quite clearly apart from the male community, but equally clearly the idea of total segregation had not yet taken root. The greater saints such as Patrick and Diarmaid wrote Bieler, "neither refused the service of women nor objected to their company. Building firmly on the rock which is Christ, they did not fear the storms of temptation!"

Gradually the original ideal faded and we find a later Synod decreeing that "A monk and a virgin, he from one place and she from another, shall not spend the night in the same inn or drive from one place to another in the same carriage or engage in long conversations", the basic idea being that prevention was the better kind of cure. In other early monastic churches the strict segregation of Inch Cleraun was not observed but a wooden partition was built down the centre of the aisle with the men worshipping on one side and the women on the other.

Another feature of the churches of this monastery is that although most of them face in an easterly direction, there is a good deal of variation. Teampul Diarmaid for example is oriented many degrees out of alignment, and the explanation is that the saint followed the Druidic custom, in the days before the invention of the compass, of pointing the centre of his altar towards the source of light. As the sun appears to rise against a different part of the earth's rim at different seasons of the year it has been nicely calculated that this little church was first dedicated and laid out some time between December and January.

Before we left that island which had played such a vital part in the evolution of Celtic mythology, we swung our boat in close to the shore of its northern peninsula called Muckinish or Pig Island, which lies a few hundred yards from Mr. Walsh's farm. The curious name of this tract of land derives, I believe, from the sacred boars or pigs which were at the heart of the Druidic Celtic worship of the fire or sun god. To comprehend the process of Druidic sacrifice we must turn to Tara as the best documented source, always remembering that the capital of Meath was only one of many religious centres where these sacrifices were carried out.

Every year on November 1 at Tara the King, who was the living incarnation of the divinity and therefore maintained the earthly fire of the sun would light, from his perpetually burning hearth, the *torc tened* or fire boar, a tall pyramid of logs, and from this flame in turn runners with fiery brands would visit all the houses of the countryside to kindle the symbolic flame of the sacred boar as the source of household warmth and food during the bleak months of the winter solstice.

All this must seem remote from Pig Island, but as hunting made the wild boars scarcer it became necessary to breed them and it was on that peninsula, no doubt once separated by an artificial ditch, that the sacred boars and sows of the local Druids were kept. Human beings were not the only creatures burned alive by the terrible servants of the god of the sun. Professor R. A. S. MacAlister, describing a discovery during the excavation of the hill-top at Uisnech, west of Tara, writes of the relics of a succession of fires:

75

. . . so hot that the ground underneath it was burnt to a red colour for some depth. Intermingled with these ashes were the charred skeletons of animals : there is no question of cooking, for nobody would allow the bones of an animal which was being cooked to be charred. There is some evidence that sacrifices which took the barbarous form of burning animals alive, lasted down to living or recently deceased memory, the purpose being to avert or bring to an end a cattle plague.

The theory has been put forward that the Celts revered hogs so deeply because the foetus of the pig closely resembles that of the human being during much of its evolution. Though the present chaos in international affairs strongly supports this interesting thesis, I am more inclined to believe that the savage bristling wild boar with his lightning speed and vicious nature was taken into their religion as the closest semblance to the sun and the fiercest and most exciting animal to hunt among the creatures of creation that were then known. The custom of sacrificing animals and even babies continued among the witch-covens of the sixteenth and seventeenth century, and was a survival of the old religion in remote country places. A former inhabitant of Inch Cleraun, Ennia Uahach, who was another sister of Queen Maeve, was described as "famed for slaughters", because on the advice of the Druids she not only sacrificed babies, but ate them as well, and a mildly superstitious person could be excused for wondering whether the Farrell's house might not have been built a little too close to that princess's sacred mound.

The gale had vanished almost as swiftly as it had risen, and waving farewell to Mr. Walsh we headed up the lake. The broadening wedge-shaped wake of the *Mary Ann* spread out astern, the strange island of the sacred pigs settled gently on to the horizon and I found myself contemplating the curious theology of the hog. Some elements of the early religion of Ireland came from ancient Egypt where the pig was a sacred animal and was used in burnt offerings to the gods, but it was also considered to be unclean and anyone who had the misfortune to touch one was obliged to immerse himself in the waters of the

Nile as an act of purification. This ritual prejudice may have
been retained by the Jews and Moslems, and probably quite
wisely in a hot climate in the days before bacon curing, when
the domestic animal was a good deal less wholesome than the
wild boar. Fortunately the prohibition failed to extend to
Christianity, though it might well have done so had not St. Peter
gone up on to a housetop at Joppa to say his prayers. As he
prayed he saw a vision descending from heaven of all the beasts
of the earth, and doubtless a pig or two among them, and
though the saint protested that he could not eat anything that
was common or unclean he was rebuked by the voice which
said: "What God hath cleansed, that call not thou common!"
So I rather fancy that we were indebted to St. Peter for the
fact that we could fry a little excellent Irish bacon in our pan
as we wended our way among the lakes and islands, and a very
fragrant scent it had too, mingling with the early morning air
by the verges of the lake.

Inch Cleraun is a strange and fascinating island where one
feels that the pagan past has not been altogether obliterated by
the message of peace and goodwill towards men which later
replaced it, and perhaps that is why local tradition holds that
St. Diarmaid's ghostly figure still guards its coast and walks the
waters round its stormy shores. When the antiquary John
O'Donovan visited the island a local boatman called Brannan
told him that he and two others had seen "clearly, plainly and
distinctly, a man of tall stature walk upon the water and tread
the waves with noble step", and they watched him until he
vanished over the sea in the direction of Athlone. This is indeed
a forgotten island, where there lingers yet some aura of the
supernatural wreathed in the spells and charms and potions of
an ancient magic.

Chapter 7

DANCING ON A LAKE

FROM Inch Cleraun we sailed between a host of islands until we began to feel the powerful tug of the current which bursts out in great strength from the confining arches of Lanesborough Bridge, and there we found a small hotel where we could rest and recuperate, for the long battering of the waves and the worries and problems of navigation in unknown waters can take a considerable toll of one's nerves. Fully laden our boat had less than a foot of freeboard at the stern which meant that we were safest when we presented the bow to anything like a sizable sea, and this had involved us in some curiously zig-zag voyages to and fro across the lakes.

Though it is a tidy and attractive place, it is hard to believe nowadays that Lanesborough was once a royal borough which returned two members to Parliament, and had a mayor, two bailiffs and twelve burgesses. There is little to indicate that it was ever much larger, and so one can take this quiet hamlet as a classical example of a pocket borough, although it also had a certain military importance as the only place for crossing the Shannon between Athlone and Termonbarry. For the passing boatman the main virtue of Lanesborough is to provide supplies and a reasonable mooring against the stone quay on the left of the river above the bridge. This jetty is now the home port of the luxurious cruisers run by the Kennedy family which carry parties of six to twelve people on week-long cruises up the navigation to Lough Key and also run archaeology voyages to visit the most famous castles and monastic settlements on the Shannon.

We felt some relief at escaping from the waves of Lough Ree and wound our way upstream against a gentle current, passing the small elongated green islands on the right-hand bank until we came to the spot where the Royal Canal drops down to join the Shannon. There is a tale in Samuel Smiles's work that this waterway was constructed through the influence of a re-

78

tired shoemaker who had invested a considerable sum in The Grand Canal Company and was a member of the Court of Directors. A bustling, interfering little fellow according to Smiles, he managed to antagonize his fellow directors because he would intervene in administrative matters which were not directly his concern. Eventually, furious at the rebuffs which he had received, he sold his shares, resigned his directorship, and flounced out of the room saying, "You may think me a very insignificant person, but I will soon show you the contrary." Thus it was said, was the rival Royal Canal across Ireland built from Dublin to the Shannon, the shoemaker lost most of his fortune in the project, and he was not the only person to suffer financially through seeking revenge on his former colleagues.

The new water way did have certain initial disadvantages. Not only was it eleven miles longer than the main line of the Grand Canal but it had fifteen more locks; quite apart from this it ran through several narrow cuttings where it was difficult for fully-laden boats to pass each other. In 1797, the first operating year, the Royal ran at a considerable loss; by 1810 the combined profit from passenger boats and from tolls had risen to £15,024, but whereas the Grand Canal had carried 205,433 tons of goods, the Royal had only coped with 52,643 tons, of which the largest single item was potatoes!

Now Smiles was a prejudiced writer and an inaccurate historian, as I have shown elsewhere,* and if, as seems likely the founder of the Royal was John Binns who was a Liberal politician of some distinction, and held important posts in local government in Dublin, then this would seem to be another example of Smiles's imagination getting the better of his facts. Nor was he correct in assuming that this waterway was a complete failure. Though never in the same category as the Grand Canal it paid a dividend for well over twenty years, it carried nearly 100,000 tons annually between 1844 and 1855, it provided a valuable passenger service in times when travel on the roads was difficult, uncomfortable, and at times dangerous, and last but by no means least it provided a means of livelihood and served the economy of the countryside through which it was

* *The Canal Duke,* David & Charles, 1961.

driven for upwards of 160 years. Its final achievement before it was closed in 1961 was to carry considerable supplies of turf to Dublin when other fuels were scarce. The Royal is no longer navigable but it runs through country which is far more attractive than the route of the Grand Canal, and it seems likely that within the next fifty years or so it will be reopened as a vital link in the triangular voyage from Dublin to the Shannon and back; I hope very much that I may survive to take a nonagenarian journey along its winding and peaceful waters, through Mullingar, Killucan, Kilcoch and the theological college at Maynooth.

The walk up to Richmond Harbour which is the Shannon terminus was well worth our trouble. It is a gem of late Georgian canal architecture which should be studied by all industrial archaeologists – a broad sheet of water winds away under a symmetrical roving-bridge to an attractive lock, while the harbour itself is lined on either side by two facing rows of simple but dignified buildings which include dwellings and warehouses. As the Royal was not completed as far as the Shannon until 1817, it was probably somewhere around that time that it was opened by the Lord Lieutenant, the Duke of Richmond, and named after him.

A little way upstream of the harbour entrance is a lock where one should keep well to the left to avoid being carried against the sluices which run out from the opposite bank, and beyond this again lies Termonbarry – now no more than a little hamlet gathered around the bridge which spans the Shannon. The holy land, sanctuary or termon of Berach was said to have been granted to him by St. Patrick himself, but when Berach returned with his pet stag carrying his books for him he found that the meadow was the scene of a great battle where two royal princes had fallen fighting each other, and their followers lay dead or bleeding to death around them, so the saint went up into the carnage of the fort and brought back to life the fighting men who had engaged in the siege. There with the aid of Presbyter Fraech and Daigh son of Cairell, the monastery was built and consecrated, but unfortunately while Berach had been away on his travels the land had been given by Aedh, King of Con-

3 Janus god of Boa Island
showing libation stoop for sacrificial blood.

4a The unique inland lighthouse, Ballycurran, Corrib

4b The Neale stones, near Cong

naught to Rathonn Diarmait, his head poet and chief master
of Druidism in payment for a magnificent poem which he had
composed in praise of his royal master.

The counter claims over the ownership of this monastery and
its land produced one of the fiercest duels in the whole of Ireland in the long-drawn-out war between paganism and the new
faith. The weapons in the hands of the Druids were mostly poetic
for they were gifted with a wonderful skill in producing pane-
gyrics of those they sought to flatter and a deadly ability at
lampooning those they hated. The following sample shows something of their capacity for satire, even in translation, and was
probably aimed at a bishop – perhaps even at St. Patrick himself :

> *Adze-head will come*
> *Across the bold-headed sea*
> *Hollow-head his mantle,*
> *Bent-head his staff,*
> *His table facing east . . .**

This kind of condemnation was the ancient equivalent to
having your name attached to a rather unsavoury incident in a
national newspaper, for even then news travelled fast, and in no
time at all the jangling lines were being repeated by the Druid
bards in every fort and banqueting-hall in the land. But the
ministers of the new faith did not go wholly unarmed themselves,
their skill in producing miracles in the nick of time being incon-
trovertibly superior to all the muttered spells and demoniacal
incantatations of the rival religion.

Consequently poor King Aedh found himself in a horrible
fix. If he gave the land to the saint he knew that Diarmait would
satirize him, and as the Druids had long memories he and his
line would go down sadly blemished to posterity : in any case
Rathonn was virtually equivalent to his prime minister. On the
other hand Berach had built his monastery and was famed for
his miracles; moreover, unpleasant things had been happening to
those who interfered with the new faith. So the King refused to
act as arbitrator, and though they searched Ireland through

*Quoted from L. Bieler, *Ireland.*

they could find no one else who would take on such a thankless task.

The litigants then took their case before Aedan, the King of Scotland, and it seems that they travelled to Aberfoyle in Perthshire, where Diarmait dressed up in his full Druid regalia but Berach said his prayers, so that the saint, who was poorly clothed was attacked by a mob of youths. As they came towards him he said quite gently, "May you be unable to do what you attempt," whereupon they were frozen in the very act of attacking him; their feet stuck to the ground, their hands were glued to the sticks which they had grabbed to beat him, and their faces remained distorted in grimaces of anger.

At the entrance to the fort lay two piled mounds of snow. "O imposter," said Diarmait, "if you were a true clerk you could make a fire blaze from those heaps of snow to keep us warm!"

"Let fire be made of them. Get up and blow them," said the saint gently. Rathonn puffed away, the heaps of snow suddenly roared up in flame as though they had been made of kindling wood and the monk and the Druid stretched out their hands to the comforting heat.

After this it was not surprising that Aedan should have given his judgement in favour of Berach, and so they returned to Ireland, the troublesome youths having been duly released, a good deal chastened by their experience, and once they were home Aedh of Connaught placed himself under the saint's protection because he feared the lampoons of his courtier. Just as the poet was about to sing out a few lines of extempore satire against the King, Berach strode up to Rathonn, put his hand over his mouth and cried out, "Neither satire nor panegyric shall cross these lips for ever, and I declare that this day one year from now shall be the day of your death!" From that time on Rathonn's inspiration never returned and he fled to the protection of Bishop Soichill, who wisely told him to stay inside the local church on the fatal anniversary predicted by Berach. Unfortunately a hunted stag stopped to get wind just outside and Rathonn could not help putting his head to the window to watch the chase. One of the hunters flung his javelin, but the stag leaped clear and the spear flew through the window, severing the jugular vein of Rathonn Diarmait, so that he died in a sanctuary of the very church which he had struggled for so long to oppose. And thus, by the intervention of providence, as the Christian chronicler notes with deep satisfaction, the land which St. Patrick had promised to St. Berach came to be held by its patron saint and by his monastery until the Vikings came raiding up the Shannon.

As we moved upstream under the bridge and out into marshy country beyond we thought of another strange legend of St. Berach, and of how the powerful Shannon O'Briens came raiding the cattle and burning and pillaging into the land of the smaller clans which were under St. Berach's protection. The saint went out against them alone and rebuked them and told them to go home, but laughing contemptuously at the absurdity of the little cowled figure they rode past him along the edge of the bog. Berach rang his bell once, the lone note tinkled out on the wind, the earth gave way beneath their feet, and the water flowed in to drown the raiders in a single bubbling wave. It is said that you can still see the entire army clad in mail with their spears on their backs and King Cucathfaid floating at their head, if you peer carefully down into the peat-brown waters. Their protruding eyes stare up still glazed with surprise at the sky which vanished so suddenly from their ken and bubbles of marsh-gas float around them like phosphorescent strings of fresh-water pearls.

Roosky is an attractive and enterprising little village where Tony Fallon was doing a useful business in hiring out cabin cruisers to visitors to the Shannon, and providing with it refreshments and a gay if somewhat deafening music which was relayed through a loudspeaker on the bank. We sailed on across Lough Bofin, where the long breakers coming from the southwest took our boat and rolled her and shook her until we were hurled into the sheltered waters beyond the Derrycarne Narrows. Normally these small lakes on the upper Shannon are tolerably smooth and free from storms but occasionally the wind sets dead against the current, and the very narrowness of the waters limits one's freedom to manoeuvre. The light was already beginning to fade a little and the twilight blended with a touch of mist here and there to delude us, but eventually we managed to pick out the markers which guard the entrance to the mysterious recesses of the Carranadoe waters.

For those who have grown bored with the crowded ways of this world the Carranadoe and Grange Navigation can be safely prescribed as a sufficiently remote retreat. We were cold, tired and hungry by this time and had been surprised and shaken by the sudden storm that had hit us at Derrycarne. Winding our way up Carranadoe we entered a weird wilderness of reed, sky and water where there was no place to land and camp so we were obliged to go on into the the gathering twilight, damp from the spray and holding our feet out of the water which had lapped over the gunwales during the gale. Though we were hardly able to appreciate it that evening, these desolate lakes have their own brand of haunting beauty, very different from the rest of the Shannon; the reed has carved varying patterns as it encroaches on the waters, so that any skipper who has studied only their mapped outline would be hopelessly deluded and lost without the guiding markers, and these, as the light faded, we found increasingly difficult to locate.

At last we moored at Ballantyne's Wharf at the far end of Grange Lough just as the early stars were winking out in a sky which the wind had swept clear, and pitched our tent in the hold of an old barge which was securely moored. In the morning Peter Connellan came down to look at his boats and asked us if we had ever heard of the Rockville Navigation, which leads away into the heart of the countryside to the north of Grange. It is a group of lakes connected by short canals, and Peter told us that he had taken his boat up it during the winter months when the Grange River was in flood, to shoot the geese which come in there to feed.

"I'll tell you what," he said. "If you're interested you can borrow my boat, put your outboard motor on the back and go up through the Rockville waterways. There are shallows on the river near here, and your own boat would draw too much to get through at this time of year, but a rowing-boat or a canoe can make it, and the lakes themselves are good and deep."

DANCING ON A LAKE

Although there is a mention of the Rockville Navigation in the excellent *Pilot Book of the River Shannon* this series of lakes was very seldom visited even by local people, and for us there was a particular fascination in exploring a waterway which was so little known. We rowed Peter's narrow Shannon skiff under the bridge and jumped out into the shallow water beyond. The clear river ran ice cold over our legs, but the sun came up from a thin mist and blazed down on our backs; we were surrounded by the music of the swirls rippling and eddying around the stones, and the flies and gnats dancing in and out of the shadows.

A double barbed-wire entanglement stretching over and under the water added the complexities of an assault course to our voyage at a point where the farmer was anxious to prevent his cattle from straying, and after that we had to wade and paddle for about 400 yards, under a bridge and through another barrier of barbed wire, until we wondered whether the local inhabitants had formed a confederacy to exclude all outsiders.

When the river grew deeper we lowered the outboard motor and moved into a cool tunnel where the branches of trees and shrubs met in an interlacing tangle over our heads, until gradually the banks began to open out into a low-lying meadow-land where huge trout, a deep shade of steely blue hesitated a moment at the threat to their solitude and then shot off suddenly into the clear water away from the threatening keel. The river wound into a small lake which we sped across, and seeing a weeded canal at the far end we charged it, rather like a blind jump; the engine hesitated and sputtered for a moment as the weed choked the propeller, but the momentum carried us through and we plunged out on to the surface of Lough Nablahy, glittering in the morning sunlight and almost encircled by low, green hills. The margin was surrounded by reeds, and it held no islands. The powerful outboard shot Peter's little skiff quickly across this open water. We encountered two more cuts, the second being both shallow and weeded before we reached the lovely Lough Dooneen with a round wooded island towards the far end, close to the original site of Rockville House.

By this time we had penetrated far into the countryside towards Elphin but the next cutting led on through a narrow gap in the reeds to a deep, round pool, small, but overhung with branching trees of great age which had the gaunt look of a petrified forest. The next canal was blocked by a fallen willow but we managed to ease the boat through a minute gap by the bank into even lovelier country where a variety of trees formed a canopy over our heads. In the heart of this cutting was a tall canal bridge with a small overgrown stone quay lying a little downstream of it. It seems probable that this natural chain of lakes was once used for carrying the turf down to Ballantyne's Wharf for transhipping to the larger Shannon barges; behind the quay rose a tall pyramidal pile of it which had been newly cut to dry in the hot sun.

Beyond the bridge lay two more lakes of which the second, Lough Nahincha, was far the loveliest with its two small islands densely matted with trees which seemed to have fought a long battle of survival to obtain a meagre hold for their roots. We tried to travel farther but could find no outlet through the reeds, though later we learned that there were two more lakes beyond Nahincha and another two branching off southwards which can still be navigated.

It was growing late, and we had spent most of the day in exploring this hidden waterway, but we returned more quickly than we had come, with the current pushing us along. Kay acted as lookout in the bow, peering down into the clear water to prevent us from running aground as we paddled the little Shannon skiff down the fast-flowing canals, watching the lazy ripple of the weed in the current and the elusive dragonflies darting and hovering over the heads of the water-lilies. On the lakes we encountered no hidden snags or shoals, though that may have been sheer good fortune, for there were no charts available, and in the whole day we never saw another boat. Long shafts of evening sunlight broke down into the depths of the water and covered the bed of the stream with a thin sheen of gold, and as we glanced down we saw a crusty, evil-looking three-foot long pike staring up at us beadily less than an arm's length below.

As the last of the sun vanished we moored alongside the old

barge and Peter Connellan greeted us from the bank, took us to his home in the fine main street of Strokestown for supper, and on to the local hotel for an evening of broadly Irish hospitality which included a drink from that farmer upon whose barbed-wire defences we had bled so profusely in the morning.

The following day as we wound our way up against the increasing power of the Shannon we met some showery weather until we moored in the Albert Lock at Drumsna, where we paused to fish and brew a little coffee. It was an uncomfortable day for oilskins and an open boat, for the gaps between the cloudbursts were extremely hot. As we glanced downstream we saw a superb rainbow curve right across the Shannon in a gigantic arch and from the centre of it came boat after boat, the first that we had seen since leaving Roosky, heading towards the annual regatta at Carrick-on-Shannon.

Leaving the faster yachts to move ahead we took our place in the line, sailed up the deep cutting which had been hewn and blasted out of living rock, and moored under the bow of an immense floating houseboat called the *Gillaroo*. We spent the night comfortably warm and dry in the nearest garage, which we gathered belonged to the hereditary chieftain of the clan O'Reilly, and the following morning set off through the series of lakes which lead to the head of the navigation. I heard it said that some of these stretches of water are haunted by ghosts which have lost their arms and, a peculiarly Irish refinement of spookiness, also seem to have lost their shirts. Apparently they have long since grown bored with frightening the belated navigator, and have evolved the maturer occupation of playing football with each other's heads.

There was a considerable gathering of boats at Carrick and later we moved upriver until the high bridge at Knockvicar loomed up before us while beyond it, through a splendour of branching trees, we saw the last lock on the navigation. Being much faster than our *Mary Ann* the other boats and yachts had passed us long before, and as we sped out on to Lough Key a shower struck it and battered the surface so hard that the splashes made it impossible to see where we were heading.

At the far end of the lake, gathered behind Bullock Island

were some forty or fifty boats, many of them gaily dressed with penants and bunting, while an array of tents and pavilions spread out across the fields by the water's edge. Tea was followed by a demonstration of water-skiing in which a number of experts skimmed gracefully over the lake behind the high-powered speedboats, approaching at times close to flying. Starting seemed to be the main difficulty, but once up they wove to and fro across the creaming wake and sailed into thin air as they struck the ripples until eventually the boat stopped and they sank very slowly into the water again. A hot sun lit the gay bunting, setting the cine-cameras and press-photographers busily to work, and as the skiing ended the yachts began to leave their moorings and turn their bows back towards Carrick while we set off to explore the loveliest of all the Shannon lakes.

Lough Key, now scheduled as a National Park, is beautiful because it has long been part of a private estate which has taken care to plant the islands with selected trees, and ensured that they were not spoiled. We landed on Bullock Island and on Hermit Island, where there are the remains of a little cell, and then came into the east side of Trinity Island, containing the ruins of a large monastery which continued to be used until the Elizabethan armies invaded this area. The general of one such army, Sir Conyers Clifford, lies buried under the branching trees. Clifford had advanced north from Boyle up the road into the Curlew Mountains in August 1599 to bring relief to his advance party which had been cut off by the O'Neill's forces in Colooney Castle, beyond the hills. As he advanced he was attacked by the chief of the clan MacDermot and Brian O'Rourke of Breffni with an inferior force which had been withdrawing before him. The charge carried the invading army away in confusion, Clifford's horse was shot under him and though he fought his way into the advancing Irish line with his sword, he was soon cut down. An officer called Markham gathered enough cavalry to cover the retreat of the Queen's army into Boyle where they held the fortified abbey which had been founded by the MacDermots, and consecrated in 1220. Clifford's head was cut from his body, and sent to the garrison at Colooney as proof of his defeat, and seeing that there was no hope of relief they decided to surrender on terms. Another interesting grave on the north-east side of the church has a tale attached to it which is curiously reminiscent of the feuding in Romeo and Juliet. Una MacDermot fell in love with the son of one of her clan's traditional enemies, the MacCostellos, but her father refused to allow her to marry him and after a while she died of a broken heart. Costello visited her grave every night until, not long after, he also died and was buried beside her.

As we crossed the bay to the east we saw the hollow turrets and empty battlements of a Gothic Revival fortress on Castle Island, where the clan MacDermot once had their main stronghold. With a good stretch of deep water between themselves and the mainland they must have felt reasonably secure from their foes, but there is no hold that is impregnable, and the ancient square tower which once crowned the little island has vanished completely.

Rockingham House, on the south shore, came as a considerable shock to us, for we were hoping that we might have a quick glance at the outside of what was probably the finest country house built by John Nash, who was the architect responsible for turning Buckingham House into Buckingham Palace, and designed Regent Street, Regent's Park, and the Marble Arch. Instead of the magnificent classical façade, all we saw was the roofless three stories of a building which had been gutted by a fire of such intensity that the outside walls were blackened by flame for some distance around each of the large, sightless windows. Strangely enough this was not the first time that Rockingham had been through an ordeal by fire, for in 1863 the whole house had been destroyed, and only the walls were left standing. Now there seemed to be no intention of rebuilding the place but Rockingham will always be worthy of a visit from those who are interested in the waterways, for it had a fascinating private canal system designed to bring turf down from the area around Loughs Fin and Keel, through a single lock to the level of the lake, emerging almost due east of Castle Island. From there the turf boats would navigate the half-mile or so across the bay until they reached the tall metal doors on the shore in front of the house, which admitted them to the shelter of a long tunnel which ran at a gentle incline all the way under the building, and emerged in the domestic quarters behind it, and several hundred yards inland. From there the turf would be taken by the footmen to feed the fires and keep the building warm and dry.

Now fire had consumed it all, and only the bare, gutted walls jutted up at the sky. We stood and looked back across the lake as the last rays of the sunset illuminated it like a series of gigantic arclights, with the dotted islands scattered across its surface, and the small waves lit with red and silver reflected from the sky. A wonderful pageant of history had gathered around a small area – the white cowled Franciscans and their predecessors recorded it in the *Annals of Lough Key*, in which generation after generation of the monkish scribes of Trinity Island chronicled the story of this land from 1014 to 1590. The clan MacDermot paid a heavy price for their opposition to the English invaders, and their lands were granted to Sir John King, whose descendant commissioned Nash to build Rockingham in 1805.

As the evening drew on we realized that if we lingered a minute longer we would be late for a dance which was being held that night on the Shannon luxury cruiser, the *St. Ciaran*, so we turned the bow back and down the river. The sky cleared of all but a few thin plumes of cloud and the sunset lit them with innumerable shades of crimson the farther we looked towards the west. The other boats had long since departed and the air was heavy with the scent of the wild flowers and clovers which riot across these meadows in summer, but there was a deep sadness about that countryside, and though difficult to analyse, it was more nostalgic than depressing, as if the age-long wars and divisions of its people had filled the very air with the melancholy of times past.

We had lingered too late over the glories of Lough Key. Gradually the last of the light went out of the sky, the early stars winked down at us, and the heavy rain which had been followed by hot sunshine began to draw upwards in patches of river mist which grew ever denser as we wound our way down into Lough Drumharlow. At first the mist lent an enchantment to the lakes around and the rising moon touched its edges with a delicate lacework of gossamer, but it grew denser, and we began to lose our way. I recalled with trepidation the alarming experience of a friend who had tried to navigate the Shannon on just such a night as that and had wandered, utterly lost, deeper and deeper into fog-bound and uncharted waters. He had concluded his sad tale with a delightful Irishism. "When the dawn came, do you know what happened?" he asked. The question was clearly rhetorical, so I merely shook my head. "The sun rose in the west!" he cried triumphantly.

We wove our way down the river in a tentative series of parabolas, seeking markers which often enough loomed up on the wrong side of the bow, but at length we climbed out of the mist on to the quay at Carrick to be told that the *St. Ciaran* had awaited our arrival before leaving her moorings so we bolted on board and changed as quickly as we could. It was indeed a rapid transformation. One moment we had been lost in deep blankets of fog on the upper Shannon, and the next we were dancing merrily to the latest tunes as we moved down river on that luxury cruiser. I was reminded of the historic stern-wheelers of the inland waterways of the United States, with their bands and ballrooms, theatres and bars, but the *St. Ciaran* was more modern, with her diesel engines, and considerably more economical to run. Eventually we cast anchor in the dark heart of Lough Boderg, and sat down to an excellent dinner.

Looking back on that dinner and dance we agreed that the atmosphere was pleasantly informal, the company excellent, and the lake mysterious and beautiful under the long white shreds of mist which were carried over it by a light breeze. The least pleasant part of it was when I was called on to give an after-dinner speech, but I talked of the beauty of the lower reaches of the Barrow Navigation, of the handful of people who, through their hard work and dedication had kept the Shannon alive so that future generations could enjoy it, and turn it, as they surely will, into the main waterway resort of western Europe. I talked of Harry Rice, who had charted the upper lakes and taken their soundings, and whose maps remain to this day the only ones to use for detailed navigation among the islands, and I hoped that some of those who were there that night would not

91

rest content with voyages on luxury liners, but would also take to the smaller boats which would enable them to explore the loveliest lake islands in the world.

Once the ominous business of speaking was over it was pleasant to relax and enjoy the dancing once again, until at length we weighed anchor in the early hours of the morning, and returned upstream to Carrick.

There we accepted the kind offer of Freddie Waterstone to give us a lift back to Coosan to collect our car. He had chartered the powerful *St. Munchin*, a large cabin cruiser, so we abandoned our practical but uncomfortable little boat and revelled in the luxury of a yacht on which one could stretch out full length on a bunk, cook on a proper stove, or sunbathe on a warm and spacious deck. In the heart of Lough Forbes, Freddie took the essential precaution of lowering the ladder over the side and then vanished into the black depths of the lake with scarcely a splash. I dithered on the gunwale of the yacht, dabbing one toe suspiciously towards what I imagined must be the fairly icy surface which was in any case far too far away to touch, thinking the while how delectably warm was the sunshine beating on my back. A far from gentle push from Kay sent me curving into the peaty depths, and when the first shock of immersion was over I began to swim down towards the bottom in the hope of finding that city beneath the waters where Irish tradition claims that some mortals are taken to feast on golden apples and quaff wine from beakers laden with jewels. Though I opened my eyes optimistically they encountered no tables groaning with rich fare, but only the tiny particles of turf in the water which rushed past one's eyes like minute meteors, and then, just as breath was running short I remembered that Lough Ree monster, and popped up towards the surface again. We passed on down the Shannon and across Lough Ree which lay intensely blue in the evening sunlight and was ruffled only by the slightest hint of a breeze.

After a comfortable night moored to the jetty off the Hodson's Bay Hotel we crossed to Coosan and then came pounding back through one of those fits of bumpy water peculiar to the southern reaches of Hare Island, and as I was at the helm it gave me great pleasure to be able to use the large *St. Munchin* to push the waves about, instead of being pushed around by them. Inevitably we were rolling a good deal as the long, white-topped breakers came running at us, and the yacht heaved heavily sideways as we struck one wave larger than the rest. An outboard motor had been laid on the cabin roof, resting firmly against a strong wooden handrail but it had not been lashed down. Suddenly Kay put her head into the cabin, looking a little white. "The outboard's fallen overboard," she shouted, and sure enough it had vanished into some 90 feet of turbulent water. I have mentioned this sad incident only as a cautionary tale for any yachtsmen who may leave valuable objects on deck which might tempt the voracious spirits of these lakes.

Chapter 8

THE PIRATE QUEEN

L EAVING our boat moored at Jamestown we drove gently westward to the city of Galway, where the combined waters of Loughs Corrib, Mask and Carra fall 14 feet to the level of the sea in Galway Bay. Corrib is the second largest inland sea in the British Isles, being some 27 miles long, and about 11 miles wide. It contains 145 islands and rocks above water, and between Inishmicatreer and Cong is over 150 feet deep. The lake was originally named after Lir, "the master of the waters", as Yeats called him, that mythological creation, part god, part wizard and part man who ruled over all the seas, but particularly over these inland navigations, and lies buried, they say, under a tall standing stone on the south-western shore of Corrib.

Galway city is fascinating because it is so foreign. A long-established trade with the continent and with Spain in particular has given it a kind of pre-historical entry to the Common Market – an atmosphere of cultural links with Europe rather than with the rest of Britain, but it has its own excellent histories and guide-books and our task lay mainly with the three inland seas which lie in the lee of the Partry Mountains and Joyce's Country. From most points along this coast one can see the main Aran Islands, Inisheer, Inishmaan, and the largest, Inishmore standing like a lost cause among the pounding seas of the Atlantic. Small steamers run out from Galway to carry supplies but it is only possible to land on Aran when the ocean is relatively calm. On the south coast of Inishmore, just opposite Killeany, stand the ruins of the Black Fort, a circular castle of unmortared masonry guarded by a maze of sharp standing stones reminiscent of tank-traps, which were set up to foil besiegers. Aran, swept by winds and lashed by waves, was the final retreat of the early inhabitants of Ireland when the Celts outflanked them and drove them west about 350 B.C. and defeated their last great leader, King Eochai at the Battle of

Moytura, which lies a little to the east of Cong on the neck of land separating Loughs Mask and Corrib.

The defending Firbolg were probably closely akin to the original Iberian inhabitants of Ireland but the invading Tuatha de Danaan caused scholars a good deal of difficulty, and were long thought of as a separate race. They are now understood to have been the pantheon of the Celtic gods, for that people had a confusing habit of attributing their victories to the gods, who, they believed, fought for and with them. In ancient Egypt also, victories were attributed to the gods: at Thebes Tuthmosis III's conquests were celebrated as those of the God Amun, while defeats were, it was held, caused by the displeasure of the tribal or national god.

Knowing that we were anxious to visit the islands on Lough Corrib Mr. Higgins kindly lent us his motor-boat and we set off down the river at Oughterard, where the freshwater mussels are said to produce the occasional pearl, and lampreys come to spawn and to die soon afterwards. We passed a long array of fishing skiffs which were built by the Kinnevy family which now lives in the village : they told me that they had been building boats for about 400 years, and had lived on the islands until some twenty years ago; they are one of the very ancient clans of Corrib mentioned in early records as burying their dead around St. Patrick's Church on Inchagoill Island.

Ahead of us lay a series of beautifully green and wooded islands of a fair size mostly standing rather higher out of the water than those on the Shannon, and as we drew towards them we butted into a sea filled with long, powerful rollers whipped on by a fresh northerly wind. Away to the west lay the crouched outline of mountains with names which survive from a pagan past – Lugnabrick, Carn Seel'in, Corcogemore and the Devil's Mother. Mountains vary enormously, and these seemed to bear little relation to the jagged, fairy-tale type that I had clambered over only a few years before in the Red Sea Hills of Egypt where there is virtually no moisture; all the same these storm-flattened uplands around Joyce's Country have a weird and distinctive character of their own. When I was taking recordings in Ireland for the B.B.C. with Jack Dillon we drove westwards

from Corrib and were admiring the long sweep of the combe some ten miles ahead of us. Suddenly, as we moved along the road, the largest glen had the sunlight blotted out of it, a small dark cloud which had gathered on the mountain seemed to swell to vast proportions, a blackness strangely tinged with mauve engulfed the valley as the mist swept down it until the bright countryside which we had admired only a minute or two before had vanished entirely. Jack muttered something about the *Dark Lady of the Glen* and it was only later when the music had been interlaced with the recordings that I realized the full significance of the Irish bagpipes playing that beautiful lament.

These mountains are seldom the same for long but change, as the clouds come storming in from the west, through every subtle shade of blue down to a deep black and the combes which run up into them might, I have often thought, reveal the more than life-sized figures of a forgotten mythology; giants, ogres, banshees, ancient armies and departed kings; you feel that if you touched some crumbling stone by mistake and muttered the wrong word a spell might yet be broken to set them marching down once again on an unsuspecting countryside.

Giving the islands a wide berth, since we had no chart of the lake, we kept well to the centre of the buoyed navigation until Inchagoill, *The Foreigner's Island*, rose out of the waves to the north. It was long and almost kidney shaped, well planted with trees, and we found good deep water until the keel ground into the pure white sand of the beach. In the days before detergents this sand was valued by the islanders for scouring out greasy pots and pans, and we spent a golden half-hour sunbathing and fishing there among the shallows.

A pretty two-storied cottage crowns the western headland but we turned east, and after walking across some disused fields reached an open space in the forest filled with the ruins of two very early churches and a small cemetery scattered with a few crumbling gravestones, while in the foreground was a square standing stone jutting up from the earth. We found two small crosses cut on all its faces except the northern one while an inscription down one side was carved in that cursive Latin lettering which the Celtic scribes created and from which our modern handwriting has evolved. Translated, the words mean simply *The stone of Lugnaedon son of Limenueh* and this would convey little enough if it was not already known that this St. Lugnath or Lugnaedon's mother was called Darerca, who was reputedly St. Patrick's sister. The chronicles claim that Darerca was married twice and bore some fifteen sons almost all of them becoming bishops or abbots while her two daughters espoused the faith and remained unmarried. At least three of her sons became saints at a time when that honour was rather more easily attainable than it is today, and one of them was Rioch of Inchbofin on Lough Ree. One cannot help sensing a hard kernel of truth somewhere in this hagiography, but whether "sister" is meant in the monastic or blood relation sense would be hard to say.

Certainly this stone bears one of the earliest Christian inscriptions and carvings of the cross in the British Isles and could hardly be later than the fifth or early sixth century; it was doubtless a pagan standing stone time out of mind before that, marking a cultic gathering-place for the local tribes and islanders. The link between Patrick and Presbyter Lugnath is further strengthened by a tradition which should make this standing stone a centre of pilgrimage for all Irish sailors, for the legends claim that he was the patron saint's chief skipper and navigator. Such traditions cannot wisely be treated as incontrovertible but there could be no fitter resting-place than that lovely island glade for the man who guided St. Patrick himself across the stormy waters of the Irish Sea and among the shoals and capes and islands of the Way of the Saints. He was in the same profession as that merchant seaman who was sailing for Britain and not as was once believed, for France, and whose wooden ship the escaped slave Patrick was able to catch in the nick of time when, divinely inspired, he had escaped from his servitude. On the lakes and rivers he would have piloted the saint in a coragh, a small boat with carefully-sewn hides stretched tightly over a wooden framework – a boat which would skim lightly over the roughest waves, rather than ploughing through them. They are still used extensively for fishing along the west coast of Ireland, though now canvas and tar have been substituted for the old skin plating.

St. Patrick's Church, though larger, resembles that of St. Dermot on Inch Cleraun, for it was aligned to the rising sun, and runs a little north of east, and south of west. It is some 34 feet long, and the outer wall is built of massive unmortared stones which must have called for considerable faith and perseverance to hew and heave into place. The narrow doorway slopes in towards the top, and is crowned by a vast lintel of solid stone. These sloping entrances often puzzle strangers, who do not realize that the men who built churches between the fifth and eighth centuries had received no Roman tuition in constructing arches. They soon learned by disastrous trial and error that even if the gap was only a few feet wide, vertical sides resulted in the weight of the masonry above crushing even the thickest lintel, so that the entire wall came tumbling down. By sloping the jambs inwards they splayed much of the weight of the roof on to the walls at the side, and so solved this primitive architectural conundrum. Doors, as we understand them, do not seem to have been employed on most of these early churches, though a mention of bolts during St. Brendan's visit to Britain suggests that they may have been in use by the ninth century, and possibly earlier; wooden boards or the leather hides of beasts killed in the chase were used to keep the frost at bay. While there is no precise record available the architectural evidence clearly suggests that St. Patrick, his trusty navigator and his small band of followers could well have lived on Inchagoill and worshipped in a wood or wattle hut, on the spot where now this little unroofed chapel commemorates his name.

Certainly the island was blessed with prosperity and a community sprang up which increased until a new sanctuary called the *Church of the Saints* had to be constructed nearby, the two buildings being linked by a flagged path 79 yards long so that on ceremonial occasions the vestments of the ministers would not trail in the mud. Though the saints' church may lack the historical sanctity of St. Patrick's, it compensates for this by the richness of its architecture. Some 38 feet long, it may well have been built by about 900 and the arched Romanesque doorway alone is well worthy of the roughest voyage across the lake. The entrance is carved from a soft, dark-red sandstone, and crowned by a semi-circular arch set with ten faces which may be portraits of the most distinguished saints, abbots and scholars connected with this ancient seat of learning. Under these, and integral with the arch lies the zig-zag stonework associated in England with Norman architecture, but what lends the doorway it's chief distinction are the heads crowning the capitals at the sides. These would seem to be warriors or kings, rather than prelates, for their hair, moustaches and beards are, in contrast with the clean-shaven figures above, plaited and interwoven like the marginal decoration of an illuminated manuscript. This braided hair covers most of the face and a good deal of the neck and being tightly matted would have offered valuable protection against the cutting edge of a sword or axe, which suggests that they were local chieftains or petty kings – possibly benefactors of the abbey – and among them no doubt representatives of the septs of the Connors and the Flaherties. The round tower of Devenish on Lough Erne carries similar figures with braided hair, possibly by the same sculptor, so that the buildings may well be of the same period. As all the carvings on the doorway are of a soft stone, the driving rains and frosts of over a thousand years have gouged out narrow but deep holes which give these dignified and strangely bearded chieftains such a pitted appearance as would be the despair and envy of any modern sculptor.

Now the Druids were head hunters in pagan times and made a special cult of decapitating their enemies, much as the Red Indians gathered scalps; these severed heads they brought home in triumph to adorn their temples, and a morbidly grisly sight they must have been. There is no doubt that the carvings on this magnificent doorway are a Christian adaptation of this earlier tradition, in a setting where there would certainly have been a pagan tribal sanctuary in earlier days.

Inside the Church and built into the wall is a very ancient cross in the Byzantine style which may commemorate one of the brethren who had travelled to the East on pilgrimage. The altar, which is in excellent condition, contains a hollow large enough to hold a clenched fist which was used as a very early font, and

was once a bullen stone for Druidic rituals. Though it must be many centuries since anyone was baptized there, we learned that Fr. Quinn of Galway had recently made a pilgrimage to the island and had celebrated there; it must have been a moving service in the roofless chapel with the lake wind rustling the leaves overhead, and probably the first since the Norsemen came raiding up Corrib, burning and looting and laying waste.

Inishmicatreer, to the east, is linked to the mainland by a causeway and had a small school where the islanders once sent their children, but though one or two wealthier people have purchased lake islands as summer resorts on Corrib, most of the islanders have either emigrated or gone on to the mainland, and there was always a danger in ferrying children to their studies in the winter over icy waters lashed by Atlantic gales – I believe that the Kinnevy family was the last to abandon its ancestral fishing grounds.

The island of Inchiquin has little left on it to remind us that Brendan the Navigator, patron of sailors and shipping and after Patrick the most renowned of Irish saints, was once a missionary there in the heart of a land of barbarous and Druidical enchantments. Brendan remains the patron of sailors because he was the first great saint to go adventuring into uncharted oceans. The early Church in Ireland sent missionaries to explore and settle on Iceland and other North Atlantic islands and it is also extremely probable that they took their little ships by devious arctic routes to the west coast of the American continent, a voyage comparable in technical achievement to a modern landing on Mars.

One motive driving these men on their hazardous voyages was the hope of actually finding the Land of Paradise. The world, which was then thought to be flat, was almost entirely unexplored and they held, not unreasonably, that there might actually be such a physical entity as the Promised Land. These Celtic monks were the most cultured scholars of their age with a broad range of classical works at their disposal which must have included the enchanting myth of The Fortunate Isles which reputedly lay some three days sailing to the west. The only link

100

between these Elysian fields and the rest of the world was a group of humble fishermen who, late at night when they had gone to bed, would hear an insistent rapping on their doors, and a ghostly voice calling to them out of the darkness. They would come down and find no one there, but strange, dark-black vessels would be anchored in the bay, and heavily laden, though there was nothing that could be felt or touched in the holds. Once the fishermen had rowed the boats to the open sea a mysterious power would take over and send them creaming on their way until they reached the Fortunate Isles where again they saw no one, but would hear ghostly voices calling each invisible passenger by name as he or she stepped off on to the shore of that beautiful and peaceful land. Thus were the souls of the departed ferried across to Paradise, and it was those same isles that Brendan the Navigator and his brethren set out to discover. One strongly suspects that the tale originated in the ancient British custom of burying their dead on islands like Glastonbury and Nun's Isle on Lough Ree, and had grown more than a little with the telling.

So the monks set off in their tiny ships and met with adventures which, like all the best sailors' yarns (and these were Irish sailors) grew and were richly embellished with the passing years! Yet the older poets and chroniclers are perfectly clear, practical and unmythological about St. Brendan's voyaging :

And they departed over the great-waved sea, and nothing unusual is related of their journeyings 'till they came to eastern Aran (Aranmore), having been two years on their voyage, and five on the former voyage, so that they were seven years altogether on the two voyages seeking the *Land of Promise*, as a certain poet has said :

> *And they found it at last*
> *In the high meads of the ocean,*
> *An island rich, everlasting, undivided,*
> *Abounding in salmon, fair and beauteous.*

It is of course to the poetry that one must look for the earliest record, for this was the verbal method of handing on historical knowledge, which the early church inherited from its Druid ancestors.

Back on Aranmore the saint and his hardy seafarers were received with such wonder and reverence as, wrote the chronicler "Christ and his Apostles might receive", so that they had surely achieved something unusual, for the men of Aran are nothing if not tough seafarers themselves.

And so these early verses claim that St. Brendan discovered his Promised Land; an island in "the high meads of the ocean". It seems to have taken him two voyages – the first a five-year affair, perhaps cruising around Greenland, the Orkneys and Iceland, and the second a rather quicker two years, for by then he knew his course better – and this may have taken him to Newfoundland, Anticosti, or even Long Island, off the Hudson, for the only significant clue that we have comes from the statement that the sea around it was *abounding in salmon*! This inevitably suggests the mouth of a large river where the salmon congregate, and a Celtic monk would unquestionably recognize salmon when he saw them.

These seafaring monks, with their fundamentalist interpretation of the scriptures may indeed have believed that they had discovered their Promised Land, although they were not, perhaps granted to see any of its inhabitants, but whatever the facts may have been it is all rather sad, for even if Brendan did discover America it was still not to be a Promised Land in the true sense for many generations – indeed, not until hundreds of thousands of Irishmen had died of hunger, while others poured westwards with their families in small and uncomfortable boats to escape the ravages of the 1846 potato famine, and the plague which followed it. For some of them at least, Canada and the U.S.A. did become lands flowing, if not with milk and honey, at least with the necessities of life. The recent comparatively rapid crossings of the Atlantic by intrepid men in rowing boats imply that you could hardly explore that ocean for seven years without discovering something. Yet if we sift the apparent realities from absurd and added myths of later date like lighting fires on the backs of whales, there is good reason to believe that the hardy monks of the Celtic Church preceded the Vinland Vikings in the discovery of the American continent.

From such speculation it is more satisfactory to return to the hard reality that after his great voyages Brendan retired to the long, green island of Inchiquin, opposite Oughterard, on Lough Corrib. This was where the King of Connaught often grazed his favourite chariot horses and there the saint set up his oratory under royal patronage and protection. The worst storms which he encountered on that inland sea must have seemed paltry disturbances compared with those he had met in the open Atlantic and many a good yarn must have been spun around his turf fire in the evenings, though only a few humps in the grass show where the saint and his followers dwelt and prayed.

One day, as Brendan was walking near the shore of Lough Corrib a poor man greeted him, saying: "O holy father, have pity on me and help me out of the servitude which I suffer at the hands of the king, for he has ruined us and our children." So Brendan grasped his walking-stick and drove it, in the name of God, into a piece of turf which was lying nearby. Then, picking it up, he broke it carefully, to reveal a pound of fine gold lying cosily inside. "Take this to the king," he said, "and it will free you from your servitude to him, and do *not* tell him who gave it to you!" And so the slave was able to ransom himself and his family from bondage, but the king, knowing well that the man was originally penniless forced him to divulge the source of his wealth. When he learned that it came through St. Brendan he feared to retain such miraculous gold and duly returned it to the Church. Soon after this Brendan moved his abbey to Clonfert, where the Ballinasloe branch of the Grand Canal goes down to the Shannon, and there in the twelfth century men built in his honour one of the loveliest late Romanesque cathedrals in the world.

Brendan's last great miracle was his noblest jest. The Munstermen came cattle-rustling across the Shannon and the saint walked out alone to reprimand them for their evil ways, but the marauders refused to listen and scornfully went their way, so he prayed a little and the whole army began to ride around in ever-decreasing circles until it returned to the place where the saint stood, and there they remained immobile until they had sworn that they would keep the peace and be of good order. Soon after this Brendan died at the ripe old age of 97, and was buried at Clonfert.

We found ourselves constricted in our exploration of Lough Corrib by the lack of a chart to give us a clear idea of the depth and location of the shoals. Luckily we never repeated our traumatic experience of being prised suddenly out of the water, but it was eery and uncomfortable to be constantly wondering what jagged rocks might lie ahead. The roughest reaches lie at the northern end of Corrib, while the southern area, though it can breed some tall waves, is much more sheltered.

Hen's Island lies in the north-western inlet of Lough Corrib, just off the southern coast of Joyce's Country, and you can see it clearly from the road to Cong. Of all the Irish castles that we came across, none was more romantic in its setting. Most of the rocky surface is covered with a very large, square tower house, and viewed from the water this keep seems to rise almost vertically from the waves; a fairy-tale fortress if ever there was one. To the north lies Mount Leckavrea and the dark hillside entrances to the silver and lead mines from which it is possible that material was taken to create that wonderful example of medieval Irish craftsmanship, the Processional Cross of Cong, with its oaken stem covered with silver and bronze plates washed in gold. It was completed in 1123 and is now in the National Museum in Dublin.

Caislean na Circe, or Hen's Island is difficult to land on in rough weather, but the castle is not in bad repair considering that it was one of the earliest mortared fortresses in the land, and possibly the earliest with a square keep. It was constructed as a joint venture by Roderick O'Connor and William, founder of the Burke family, but by 1225 the O'Flaherty had taken it, for the Chief Justice of Ireland ordered Odo O'Flaherty to hand it back, with all the boats on the lake to Odo O'Connor, King of Connaught, who was Cathal Redfist's* son, as a surety for peace. The tangled web of shifting loyalties had veered again

*The Cathal Mor of the wine-red hand who is mentioned later in connection with Ballintubber Abbey.

by 1256 when Walter Burke first Earl of Ulster went plundering and rustling into Connaught, stormed the castle, and took possession of the entire lake, its islands, ships and fortresses. By the sixteenth century it seems to have been back in the proprietorship of the O'Flaherty when that redoubtable colleen Grace O'Malley, who lived from about 1530 to 1600 held the castle and defended it ferociously against the Joyces, a Welsh family which had carved themselves a private barony in the rocky land between and to the west of the two lakes. Grace was married first to Domnall O'Flaherty of the lakeside castle on the long, narrow Ballinahinch Lough, some fifteen miles west of Corrib, on the main road from Galway to Clifden, and he was a ninth cousin of Sir Murtagh O'Flaherty, the head of the clan, whose headquarters was at Augnanure Castle, near Oughterard.

Grace was a termagant tomboy who wore her hair cropped and came of the wildest stock in Ireland, for the O'Malleys were sea-rovers who maintained themselves largely by piracy on the ocean islands to the west, and went raiding for a living anywhere from the mainland to the Atlantic approaches to Europe. So Grace was brought up chiefly in the wild bailiwick of her clan – Clare Island, Inishbofin, Inishturk, Inishark and Caher Island. There is a Grania (or Grace's) Castle at Kinnahooey on Clare Island, and another at the mainland headquarters of the clan close to a small lake, south of Louisburgh; Hen's Island is said to have been renamed as a consequence of her spirited defence of the fortress. What exactly happened to Domnal O'Flaherty is uncertain, but Grace married, secondly, Richard Burke, who became head of the Mayo branch of his family in 1582.

In the best Maeve tradition Grace set herself up as a pirate queen of the western isles. She failed to pay her taxes, plotted continuously against the Elizabethan ascendancy and was a law to herself. She had four children – two sons by her first marriage and one by her second, and her daughter's son was a distinctive character known to the Irish by the charming soubriquet of *The Fiend of the Sickle,* and to the English merely as the *Devil's Hook,* possibly in honour of some particularly gruesome weapon which he favoured.

Grace became a terror to the shipping lanes, leading

expeditions and boarding parties at a time when piracy and slaving were regarded as strictly the prerogative of the English, and virtually a West Country monopoly. Though captured and taken to Dublin she was later released, but when her second husband who had been something of a restraining influence died, the buccaneering queen ran wilder than ever.

About 1586, with a thousand cows and mares, presumably mostly rustled, she retreated on her castle at Borrisowle in County Mayo, where she was seized by Sir Richard Bingham who accused her of plundering Aran Island, tied her up with a rope and built a gallows to hang her, but Richard Burke sent a messenger with a pledge which saved her life in the nick of time. In his correspondence Bingham described her as the "notable traitress, and nurse of all rebellions in the province for forty years". During the days of her prosperity she is said to have visited Queen Elizabeth, who later granted her the royal pardon after she had been involved in yet another plot, and was stranded with the O'Neills in Ulster, with all her ships destroyed. Soon after her capture by Bingham she pleaded to Elizabeth's minister, Burghley, for a restitution of enough of her estates to maintain her, but that acute politician was not to be charmed, and Grace O'Malley died, it was said, in great poverty. An early protagonist, if not of Ireland's freedom, at least of the liberty of the fighting O'Malleys, she has taken her place in Irish folklore.

There are many songs about this pirate queen, and wild tunes set to the Irish pipes and fiddles, and her skull is preserved, in the best Druidic tradition, on Clare Island within a sound of the raging Atlantic storms which she had so often ridden out when she led her little wooden ships to war. One day an enterprising composer may set the tale of this, the greatest fighting colleen since Maeve to the music of an opera which would do justice to her strange saga of war and love and intrigue.

Chapter 9

THE CANAL THAT VANISHED

T HE Corrib Navigation boasts two unique attributes, the only lighthouse on an inland waterway in the British Isles, and a canal which vanished altogether. The lighthouse, which marks the rocky shoals of the Ballycurran peninsula opposite Oughterard stands about 24 feet high, is built of stone, and has the remains of a spiral stairway running up the outside to a chamber on top. The ruins of a keeper's house on the landward side suggests that the light was regularly maintained as a guide to the steamer services and would have been invaluable during heavy squalls, snowstorms, or when the lake was cloaked in fog; for these ships took three hours to navigate the lough even in fine weather, and had to follow a tortuous course among the islands.

Our headquarters on Corrib was a field by the bank of the little river Oewnriff at Oughterard. It was aesthetically enchanting enough, within a sound of the stream tumbling over the shallows, but the weather, which had been reasonably generous by Irish standards began to turn, and the bitter coldness of that place is engraved on our memories. Camping in Ireland is practical and sensible if you take the right equipment and can tolerate rain – after all, people camp year after year in the Antarctic – but one has to make allowance for the average temperature being a little lower in summer. Except in the most exposed places the lake islands are kept warm by the surrounding water but further inland at Oughterard we were not fully equipped for that icy wind which sprang up just before dawn.

The cot, a long, narrow and unwieldly hollowed log was the first boat to be used on Irish lakes and rivers, and as the earliest crannogs, or man-made islands were built around 2,500 B.C., they probably first came into service about that time, and were propelled by spear-shaped poles which could be used as paddles in deeper water. Technological progress being a good deal slower in the pre-jet age, they remained in general use right through the period of the island monasteries and on to the seventeenth century. In the club at Enniskillen we saw a drawing of the siege of that town by the Elizabethan army and it depicts these dug-outs ferrying English troops across the river for the assault on Castle Maguire. Each cot is propelled by two almost naked Irishmen, one in the bow and the other in the stern, while the troops stand sharply to attention between them, muttering, one suspects, some pretty imperialistic remarks about the native transport system.

The coracle probably evolved at about the same time as the dug-out, but the coragh was a great advance in boat technology, and in the centuries before the introduction of the pound lock it could be carried without difficulty over the shallows in the same way that the fishermen of the west coast hump it over their heads today. It survived on inland waters until mid-Victorian times, when it was superseded by the long, narrow, clinker-built skiff which can be rowed or used with an outboard; I have even seen the islanders using a small sail on these boats, but I would certainly not advise this for the uninitiated, for they have no depth of keel. These skiffs ride the waves comfortably and need little maintenance but I have often wondered how a coragh would perform on the lakes.

We know that naval battles were fought on these inland seas. ranging from Brian Boru's defeat of the Danes on Lough Ree to the confiscation of the O'Flaherty's vessels on Corrib, in which prevention was clearly the better part of the cure; in construction these vessels probably reflected the type of warship in current use on the oceans, though they were built on a smaller scale. But the craft which was most often seen on the Irish waterways down the centuries was a broad-beamed wooden boat generally rowed from the bow with perhaps an extra hand wielding a punt-pole at the stern, and carrying an absurdly large pile of heaped-up turf, until the little vessel was loaded well below any plimsoll line that the imagination could begin to consider as safe. A few of the larger turf-boats were honoured with a canvas lugsail, and they were built locally from native timber. From these there evolved a sloop-rigged vessel capable of sailing close to the wind and carrying about 50 tons of turf. I had seen the last of these, *The Sandlark*, in Garrykennedy Harbour on Lough Derg, and was told that though they were useful and economical to run on the lakes, they tended to be held up by contrary winds on the narrow river reaches of the Shannon.

Steamships were brought to the Irish waterways by John Grantham, a retired cavalry officer and a distinguished civil engineer, whose memorial in Killaloe Cathedral was raised by his friends to remind posterity of his work in surveying the Shannon and of his "having been the first who introduced steam navigation on its waters in the year 1825." This first ship, the *Marquis Wellesley*, was built by the Horsley Coal & Iron Co. at Tipton in Staffordshire, had a central paddle, and did yeoman service for some thirty years. Trading mainly between Killaloe and Banagher she carried many of the immigrants down the river during the desperate years which followed the 1846 famine. The largest steamer was *The Lady Lansdowne*, whose submerged remains were discovered by Mr. and Mrs. Delany in shallow water by the quay of the Lakeside Hotel at Killaloe on Lough Derg. She was 136 feet long, nearly 23 feet beam, of 300 tons, and powered by a 90 h.p. engine. In service about 1833, she was one of a fleet of nine steam vessels operated by Grantham's and C. W. Williams' Inland Steam Navigation Co. in the halcyon days of the waterways, before the railways took over the passenger trade.

On Lough Corrib steam was introduced in 1852 with the *O'Connell* and the *Enterprise* and since the roads around the lake were none too good these ships provided a valuable service for both passengers and merchandise. *The Eglinton*, an iron boat of 67 tons, the *St. Patrick* and the *Countess of Cadogan* followed to provide a steamer service which continued until about 1920 when the last lakeside tracks were being turned into modern surfaced roads. Sailing from Galway they ran north through Friar Island cut, the earliest canal in Ireland, which was built before 1150, and their ports of call included Annaghdown Quay, Augnanure, Kilbeg, Ballycurrin, Cong and the remote Maam Bridge on Joyce's River to the north-west of Hen's Island, so that an excellent service was provided all around the lake. Goods were loaded on to these steamers in Galway harbour, which was linked to the lakes by the Eglinton Canal, opened by the Lord Lieutenant, the Earl of Eglinton, in 1852.

Cutting this canal through the centre of the city was a costly business, for wherever roads crossed it swivel bridges had to be installed. These iron bridges were built by the engineer and iron-master Robert Mallet, but in 1956 his work was replaced by fixed spans which have completely blocked the navigation and severed the vital connection with the sea. On the Shannon the main battle over keeping the navigation open was also fought around similar bridges which he had constructed, though there it was fortunately won. As Mrs. Delany wrote, "The heritage of the 1840–50 works was almost lost for the sake of saving a few thousand pounds on fixed bridges."

In the greatest age of engineering in Ireland when the canals, railways, viaducts, aqueducts and lighthouses were being built, John Mallet, who came to Dublin from Ash in Devon, and his son Robert provided a remarkable constructional service to their adopted country. As a younger son John had to make his own way in the world, and built up a foundry for casting iron, brass and copper, which prospered enough for him to send Robert, who was born in 1810 to Trinity College where he read engineer-ing. In 1831 he took a partnership in his father's business with particular responsibility for the Victoria foundry, and built it into an extremely prosperous concern which in the words of the Dictionary of National Biography, "ultimately absorbed all the engineering works of note in Ireland." Robert's early engineer-ing achievements included raising the height of the 133-ton roof of St. George's Church at Dublin and drilling an artesian well and building steam barrel-washing machinery for the Guinness brewery. In 1836 he constructed the cast-iron swivel bridges on the Shannon, which may have been in part designed by a brother of Cecil Rhodes. In 1841 he surveyed the River Dodder at his own expense, in the hope of providing Dublin with a better supply of drinking water.

Then came the great railway boom from 1845–48 and though it was set against the tragic backcloth of the potato famine Robert was kept immensely busy building the terminal stations, engine sheds and workshops, as well as the Nore viaduct with its 200-foot span and girders 22 feet deep which we had sailed under at the beginning of our voyage. He also found time to construct the Fastnet Rock lighthouse from 1848–49 and invented and patented a special metal plate for flooring bridges which was used in the construction of Westminster Bridge and in other spans around the world. During the Crimean War he cast two immense mortars for firing 36-inch shells, but Sebastopol was taken before they could go into action.

Lady Ferguson has left a brief portrait of Robert in her memoirs of her husband :

> "He was a man of Science, and had resided for many years before he settled in London, at Delville, Glasnevin, a house which had belonged to Dean Delany, and had been decorated by his accomplished wife, whose published letters give an animated picture of Dublin Society in pre-Union days. Swift was a frequent guest at Delville, and in a summerhouse yet standing in its grounds printed the "Drapier's Letters".* Mr. Mallett, whose work on Earthquakes established his reputation in science, had a fine literary taste. His house in London was hospitably open to his friends, and to it his conversation was a strong attraction."

By 1861 the Victorian economic boom was drawing to its close, few canals were being built, and many of the main railways were already laid. Foundry work grew scarcer, and Robert was anxious to be closer to The Royal Society, since he had been elected a fellow in 1854, so he sold his business interests and set up as a consulting engineer and editor of technical magazines, with his headquarters at a house in Surrey which he called Enmore in memory of the family castle near Bridgwater in Somerset. There he produced the main body of his most valuable scientific research on earthquakes and seismology, working in partnership with his son, John; and in July 1878 he was writing to Sir Samuel Ferguson regretting that he could not attend the meeting of the British Association in Dublin, and

---

*Though this was popularly believed when Lady Ferguson was writing it is not generally held to be historically accurate.

reprimanding the geological speculators of his time. "Geology in our day," he wrote, "would present a more hopeful outlook if a larger number of its professed cultivators were better acquainted with mechanics, physics, and chemistry." Quite apart from the bridges, much of the ironwork on the Irish waterways must have been cast at the Victoria works, or by its associated concerns.

During the famine years another canal was built to link Lough Corrib with Lough Mask and provide through navigation to Lough Carra, some forty-four English miles by water from Galway. This was undertaken as poor relief, and the labourers were paid 4d. a day. We saw the bed of the waterway at Cong, cut deep into the living rock, the high bridges allowing plenty of room for the steamers which were never destined to pass beneath them. Excavation began about 1854 and despite the considerable amount of labour available, was not completed until some five years later; meanwhile broad quays with costly stone bollards were being built at Caher on the east coast of Lough Mask, and at Tourmakeady on the west. The little River Robe was dredged up to the town of Ballinrobe to take steamers at the harbour which was constructed there, and then the sluices of the canal which linked the two lakes were opened.

The water came gushing down the channel and the people at the Cong end waited optimistically for it to arrive and in a sense you may say that they have been waiting ever since, for scarcely a drop of it did they ever see at that end. The engineers who had planned the cutting had not allowed for the porous limestone seam which ran along part of the bed. The water rushed a little way down the canal and vanished through small cracks and crevices into the endless labyrinths of underground caverns which honeycomb the land between the lakes. It was said that if the cut had been made a few miles to the east there would have been no seepage, and though a solid iron bed would have held water it would have been far too expensive to install. Modern technology offers a simple solution in a specially prepared bitumen which could be used to coat the bed of the canal, and open it to traffic for the first time in its history. Loughs Mask and Carra are linked by a short channel known optimistically as The Keel Canal which can be used by small

5a Yeats' Lake Isle of Innisfree, Lough Gill.

5b The Saints' Church, altar and doorway, Inchagoill Island, Corrib.

6 Druidic and Christian sculpture showing attributes of the White Island gods.

boats, so that if gates could be fitted at Cong and the Fives Court removed, boats would be able to lock up towards that magical green lake at the head of the navigation.

Despite the waste of money and labour at Cong, Mask was used for years by trading barges carrying corn to the Kenny Mills at Ballinrobe. One other small canal in the Corrib Navigation is the Moycullen, which was mainly a drainage channel for Loughs Ballycuirke and Pollalahy, though it also carried turf boats to supply the large houses at Deerfield, Drimcong and Danesfield, and provided a pleasant retreat for fishing and for shooting wild duck in the winter. The cost to the government of that time of some £87,000 for the main works on the Corrib Navigation was a reasonably sound investment. Goods and passengers were carried for some seventy years on Corrib and for about twenty years goods alone were carried on Mask, for a capital outlay of a little more than £1,000 a year which, despite a decrease in the value of money, is a small investment when compared with only a few miles of modern highway which would certainly not last so long or demand so little maintenance.

It would be impossible to find space to describe the many fascinating early churches, tower houses and abbeys which cluster on the margins of these lakes but alternatively one cannot leave Corrib without a brief mention of Augnanure, the ancient castle which stands guard over the shore, a little south-east of Oughterard. This is no mere peel-tower, but even in its shattered condition stands out clearly as one of the great fortresses of Ireland with flanking towers, a tall keep still over 60 feet high, a richly-carved banqueting-hall and the little river Drimeen flowing directly under it to supply its moated defences.

Though built by the Burkes, it was generally in the hands of the O'Flaherty, who was the lord of West Connaught, and this was the headquarters of his clan. There lived the chieftain surrounded by his small court, with his bodyguard, his dependent chiefs coming in to visit and consult him, his priests, his genealogist, his doctors, poets, master of the revels, tax-collectors, bee-keeper, standard-bearers, men-at-arms and charioteers. The modern country gentleman survives in an establishment which has evolved down the centuries from these baronial halls and as he struggles to maintain his own with two or three aged staff he may well envy the service provided for the O'Flaherty. Yet a chieftain's life was not altogether attractive, for his main policy lay in increasing tribal territory at the cost of neighbouring clans, and settling old blood feuds with a further killing or two, so that his existence was often brutish and short, and it was not without reason that the prosperous little trading city of Galway had, carved over one of its gateways the simple legend, *"From the ferocious O'Flaherties good Lord Deliver us."*

Cong Abbey was long called a royal foundation because it was founded by the O'Connors who were for a while the High Kings of Meath as well as local kings of Connaught. Inevitably it gathered a rich and intriguing crop of possessions. The magnificent processional Cross of Cong was built to contain a fragment of the true cross under a piece of rock crystal, and is now in the National Museum in Dublin; the King's Blood, a handkerchief soaked in the blood of Charles I after his execution was being used for curing scrofula up to the nineteenth century when Fr. Patrick Prendergast, the last to hold the ancient office of Abbot, died in 1829. St. Patrick's bell was presented by Sir William Wilde to the Royal Irish Academy and is made of iron mixed with other metals; it seems old and worn enough to be quite probably genuine. When the Abbey was destroyed in Tudor times the bell passed to the Gerarty family who lived near Ballinrobe, and was often taken up to Croagh Patrick to be kissed by the pilgrims, or, for a charge of 2d. would be passed three times round the body as a cure for rheumatism. At the time of the famine the keeper of it had to sell it to raise sufficient money to pay his fare to America.

Then there is the box or shrine which is supposed to have contained St. Patrick's tooth. It is finely carved in brass, silver and gilt with a scene from the crucifixion, and four (originally five) figures holding books, shrines and croziers which represented St. Brigit, St. Patrick, St. Columcille, St. Brendan and St. Benen; it was made for the Birmingham family in the 14th century and is studded with crystals, amber and semi-precious stones. About 1820 this wonderful piece of craftsmanship came into the hands of a man called Reilly who travelled about earning a living by curing sick people and cattle with it until one day he met Abbot Prendergast, who asked to see it. "Whose is it?" asked the Abbot. "It belonged to the canons of Cong," said Reilly. "I am the last of the Augustinian canons of that monastery, and I'll keep it," said Prendergast, and he rode away with it! After various adventures it was presented to the Academy by a Dr. Stokes.

Roderick O'Connor, the last High King of Ireland, who was born in 1116, died at Cong Abbey in 1198. He succeeded as King of Connaught in 1156 and as High King he ruled at Tara from 1166, but was defeated by Richard Strongbow and his Norman–Welsh followers and was obliged to make a treaty with Henry II of England. He never really submitted to English suzerainty and was deposed, so he made his way to Cong Abbey to spend some fifteen remaining years in its monastic peace. There he died and his body was taken to Clonmacnois on the Shannon, to be buried in the royal enclosure. T. W. Rolleston wrote his requiem:

> *Darkly grows the quiet ivy,*
> *Pale the broken arches glimmer through;*
> *Dark upon the cloister garden*
> *Dreams the shadow of the ancient yew.*
>
> *Peace and holy gloom possess him,*
> *Last of Gaelic monarchs of the Gael,*
> *Slumbering by the young, eternal*
> *River voices of the western vale.*

Chapter 10

YEATS, TARA AND THE BOYNE

THE area around Cong is famous for its caves, some being natural, while others are man-made. The fogous were built by the Iberians who fought their last great battle against the Celtic invaders about a mile to the west of the town, at Moytura. Like the early Cornish they dug long, narrow trenches in the ground, covered them with broad slabs of stone filled over with earth, and rather like squirrels used them for storage and as safe retreats against a hostile world. Some of these fogous have inner chambers approachable only by clambering up through a narrow aperture which could be easily defended by a single person.

A visit to The Pigeon Hole Cave is a good way to catch a glimpse of one of the underground waterways which supply Corrib from the upper lakes in winter. It lies about a mile west of Cong, and we borrowed a bicycle lamp from the cottage and followed a pretty path through the woods until we reached a deep pit with steps leading down sharply into the darkness. At the bottom we shone the torch around a cleft which stretched some 120 feet from end to end and was about 30 feet across at the widest point. The roof is high, with a fine cluster of stalactites at one corner, alas partly smashed by vandals. On the left lies a pool of crystal-clear water which is all that remains in the dry summer months of this section of underground river, though it becomes a swirling torrent in winter, and I peered into the depths in the vain hope of glimpsing some of the blind white trout which haunt this network of caverns. They are, of course, Druid maidens in disguise, and a British trooper who was rash enough to hook one for his dinner and popped it into the frying pan, suddenly discovered that he had a ravishing and mildly singed colleen floundering around in his camp fire with nothing on. After investigation she turned out to be a princess and he courteously returned her unimpaired to the river; even by

116

Irish standards the tale sounds mildly improbable, but the myth suggests strongly that these fish were sacred to the Druids. The Pigeon Hole can be explored for some distance, while Bally-maghaney Cave is for the more serious potholer, though I would not care to be very far down either when heavy rain was raising the water level in the upper lakes. Human skeletons found deep inside some of these caverns, combined with the fogous, helps one to understand how the leprechaun pops up suddenly in the remoter places in Ireland, for the word simply means a little person, and these were perhaps the last troglodytes of a vanquished race.

We passed Lough Mask House where a new word entered into the English language when Captain Charles Boycott's tenants went on strike and refused to post his mail, shoe his horses, gather the harvest or supply him with provisions. Boycott, who was Lord Erne's agent was the object of a policy of passive resistance advocated by Parnell in 1880 and at one stage his provisions had to be brought to the house under a cavalry escort of the 15th Hussars, from the quay at Cong, where they were landed by the Corrib steamship service.

Lough Mask is a broad lake boasting a monster which has been seen with surprising regularity down the years; indeed, it was being described in detail long before the one in Loch Ness had ever been heard of. In 1684 there was a struggle between the Dovarchie, or water-dog, as it is called locally, and a man accompanied by his powerful Irish wolfhound. Though the creature escaped it died of its injuries, and was found in a cave in the springtime, when the water level fell. A more vivid description of 1846 tells how a man walking near the lake saw the head of a beast swimming along some way out, but took no notice of it because he thought that it was an otter. The Dovarchie swam under water and emerging suddenly seized him by the elbow and dragged him in. The victim caught hold of a sharp stone and used his knife so effectively that the beast made off. He described it as being about the height of a greyhound, with black, shiny skin, and he thought that it had no hair. Despite such tales one has never heard of anyone who bathed at the pleasant sandy beach on this lake suffering any sudden attacks, though there was another clear sighting of the creature only a few years ago.

Certainly of all the places where a Dovarchie would be most likely to survive there could be none more probable than the lakes around Cong with its complicated labyrinths of underground waterways and its legendary swallow holes connected with the distant waters of the Atlantic, for a mammalian creature which needed air would find plenty to breathe among the chains of underground caverns.

Mask contains several islands of considerable interest, and though we could not visit them all we learned that Inishowen had some ruins on it. The Earl's Island at the southern end of the lake took its name from Edmund Burke, the young heir to the Earl of Ulster, who was abducted one night by his enemies from the Friar's House at Ballinrobe, taken to Lough Mask Castle and then to another fortress at the southern end of the lake, and finally murdered for obscure political reasons on the island which commemorates in his title an age of bloodshed and internecine warfare.

Inishcoog is no longer strictly an island as drainage has now linked it to the mainland but it has some monastic ruins close to the water's edge. Towards the close of the sixth century Eoghan Beil, King of Connaught, was holding court there in his fortress when he was paid a social visit by St. Cormac, who arrived in the accepted Christian fashion, looking extremely poor and scruffy, and consequently was not received with the honour which he considered to be due to the servants of God. Cormac predicted that the royal stronghold would soon cease to be a seat of kings and would become a place of prayer, and his prophesy came true, for he himself is said to have founded the monastery there. In one of the remaining walls is a small square doorway which must be part of an earlier church, for the rest is of a finer construction, dating from about 1300. By the shore stands a square structure containing two long chambers with pointed arches at the entrance. This building long proved a sore puzzle to archaeologists until Professor MacAlister identified it quite definitely as a rather primitive Turkish bath; the Celtic monastery at Tintagel in Cornwall had a very similar sweat house close to the later Norman chapel. The one on Inishcoog was set hard by the old level of the lake to enable its devotees to follow up with a cold dip. The sweating process must have eased the weary life of many an arthritic saint and particularly of those more ascetic brethren who were given to reading their breviaries half way out to sea with the water lapping around their elbows – indeed many of the legends of these sanctified immersions must stem from this same bathing custom.

Inis Eoghain is linked in summer with Inishcoog, and contains the remains of a small fortress which is surely the headquarters of that inhospitable king. The remnants of a circle of standing stones suggests that there was a Bronze Age occupation similar to that on Boa Island, the 'magic ring' being the local version of the modern parish church. On one side of the fort is a deep defensive fosse, while a broad view of the lake opens up on the other, with the cloud-capped western mountains brooding in the distance.

Most fascinating of all the isles of Mask is Devenish, which is partly man-made, and crowned by the crumbling masonry of one of the earliest mortar-built keeps in Ireland. Hag's Castle still has walls some seven feet wide at the top and considerably splayed out at the base; it encloses an area some 90 feet across, and was clearly built along the lines of a traditional Irish dun or fortified farmhouse well before the English invasions brought thousands of the more sophisticated mortared tower-houses to the land. Its founder may have been a travelled man who had visited Rome or the Holy Land and seen fortifications there, but alternatively this could have been, like the Black Fort on Aranmore, a final retreat of the vanquished race which was later rebuilt in mortared style.

In 1195 Cathal MacDermot came cattle rustling into Connaught and used Hag's Castle as headquarters for his plunders, and in Elizabethan times Sir Richard Bingham the Governor of Connaught and scourge of the O'Malley captured and destroyed the fortress at a time when it was reputed to be the strongest castle in the province.

From Mask we moved on to Lough Carra at the head of the

119

navigation, and when we caught the first glimpse of its waters we rubbed our eyes and wondered whether we had eaten something indigestible, for the entire lake was a vivid green in colour; later on we learned that this was the effect of the waves stirring up the local sediment of lime marl.

By the headwaters of Carra stands the cruciform, greystone abbey of Ballintubber, founded in 1216 by Cathal O'Connor King of Connaught, who was known as Cathal Mor of the wind-red hand. There, in a richly carved tomb lie the mortal remains of Grace O'Malley's son, Theobold de Burgo, first Viscount Mayo who clearly inherited his mother's Celtic love of the sea for he was known as Theobald of the many ships. Yet even the possession of that hereditary private navy did not offer him sufficient protection against those troubled times for he was murdered just outside this monastery by his own brother-in-law, Diarmeen O'Connor. Ballintubber means the well of St. Patrick who is said to have baptized some of his earliest converts nearby, and this is, so far, the only one of these lake monasteries to have been restored and brought back into service again since their general destruction in the seventeenth century.

Father Thomas Egan whose driving energy and remarkable gift for public relations achieved this splendid restoration, had retired to the little parish of Ballintubber for quiet and relaxation following a very serious illness and a major operation.

Far from resting he soon fell under the spell of the stirring story of this royal foundation and after some three years of research he decided to take the plunge and publish a booklet on its history at his own expense. To his amazement this work ran to four printings and has already sold 40,000 copies all around the world: "I had exactly £62 in the kitty when we began," he explained to me, "and total restoration costs for which I was and am responsible amounted to something in the region of £55,000." All but £10,000 of this he has now managed to pay off and the work is almost complete.

This remarkable fund-raising project was always ecumenical, with gifts flowing in from people of all denominations and of none – the architect was a member of the Church of Ireland while one of the leading archaeologists investigating the site was

an Episcopalian from Chicago. Finally, one rainy day in August
the Poet Laureate, Mr. C. Day Lewis drove over to Ballintubber, was shown around by Father Egan and was promptly
pinned down to writing the lines which capture so uniquely
that ecumenical spirit of peace and tranquillity that lingers
about the crumbling stones of all these lake and island
monasteries.

At the head of Lough Carra the royal abbey stands
Huge as two tithe-barns: much immortal grain
In its safekeeping, you might say, is stored.
Masons and carpenters have roofed and floored
That shell wherein a Church not built with hands
For seven hundred and fifty years had grown.

A 17th-century crucifix, austere
Stonework — they take the eye: the heart conceives
In the pure light from wall to whitewashed wall
An unseen presence, formed by the faith of all
The dead who age to age had worshipped here,
Kneeling on grass along the roofless nave.

And what is faith? — the man who walks a high wire,
Eyes fixed ahead, believing that strong nets
Are spread below — the Hands which will sustain
Each fall and nerve him to climb up again.
Surefoot and stumbler, veteran or tiro,
It could be we are all God's acrobats.

Broaden that high wire now into a bridge
Where all Christ's children meet over the fell
Abyss and walk together: let them go
Brothers in faith, not wranglers arguing through
Each step and slip on the way. May such religion
Grace your old abbey by St. Patrick's well.

Up-end that bridge. It makes a ladder now
Between mankind and the timeless, limitless Presence,
Angels ascending and descending it
On his quick errands. See the ladder's foot

121

IN THE WAKE OF THE GODS

Firm-planted here, where men whisper and bow
Like the Lough Carra reed-beds in obeisance.

From

The Abbey That Refused to Die
by C. Day Lewis.

As we returned through that land of rocks we realized how the entire basis of that countryside is founded upon and created from stone. Long, short, square, rounded and weathered by frost, they stretch to the horizon like a petrified sea, and as in the Dorset uplands one has the sensation that the people who inhabited this country in earliest times are closer and almost more tangible than those of the present day. Cairns and tumuli mark the prehistoric battlefield and the little stonehenges clustered around illustrate the gradual evolution of Irish theology. Most fascinating of all are the sculptured stones called The Gods of the Neale which were probably discovered in a local cave; there are three carvings, one of a human, one of an animal, and the third of a so-called "reptilian" creature.

Antiquarians once held that the animal was the sacred Druidic bull, the human some kind of sun-god, while the reptile was beyond explanation – indeed one wonders how it arrived in snakeless Ireland unless it was a remote cousin of the Dovarchie of Lough Mask.

The explanation is, I believe, very much more fitting. The stone comes from a Celtic monastic church and the animal, clearly a unicorn, is trying to prance on its hind hoofs like the later supporter to the royal arms which was introduced by James I, but the sculptor ran out of room, so that the carving looks more like a bull that has come to grief while climbing a tree! The unicorn, which occurs frequently in the Old Testament was a symbol of ascetic virginity in the early Middle Ages, and therefore particularly appropriate for a monastery. The human figure dissolves most probably into the angel in Revelation 7 who rose on his wings out of the east carrying the Seal of the living God and then called aloud to the four angels who had been given power to ravage land and sea:

122

Do no damage to sea or land or trees until we have set the seal of our God upon the foreheads of his servants.

The folds of his stole are clearly visible and so are the wings, though these are not shown correctly in the illustration in the local guide-book.

Finally, the 'reptilian' creature on the lower slab is by no means as cold-blooded as has been imagined, for this is none other than the lion of St. Mark, and the traditional symbol of that gospel, the 'scales' around his neck transformed into a rugged mane, or possibly folded wings. With his vicious claws, bared teeth and swishing tail he is clearly hot on the trail of some early Irish sinner.

These ancient stones, sculptured perhaps in the ninth century, stand in the grounds of The Neale House and are crowned by a readily decipherable inscription and the base of an old wayside cross dated 1526. The Neale was probably the first eighteenth-century house to be built in County Mayo and has nothing whatever to do with the Gods of Felicity, as scholars once believed. The word is derived from an entirely different Gaelic source, 'an aill' meaning the crag, or rock, which was a noticeable feature of the site on which the house was constructed. Not far away the first Lord Kilmaine built, about 1760, a copy of the temple of Apollo at Athens. The Kilmaines and the Binghams were among the earliest Elizabethan settlers in this area, and though there was a tower-castle on this site before the present house was built, no trace of it remains, since all the stones were incorporated in the new building.

Originally the temple contained a lead statue of Apollo, but this was stolen by the Fenians about 100 years ago to melt down into bullets to shoot the landlords. At the same time they removed the cupola roof of the building, and all the roof-lead from The Neale House; though the house was covered again, the temple was left open to the sky.

County Mayo is one of the last places in which one would expect to find the pyramid which lies nearby, but this is another of those delightful 'follies' which were constructed in the eighteenth century to make the grounds of country houses more

interesting. Lord Kilmaine has explained to me that it is a minia-
ture model of one of the Egyptian pyramids, and was built from
plans drawn by a relation, the Earl of Charlemont, who had
travelled in Egypt and in other parts of Africa and Asia. "The
pyramid," he writes, "does not appear on the estate maps until
1782. It must therefore have been made considerably later than
the temple." It seems to have been built over an early burial
mound traditionally associated with Slainge, the son of King
Eochai, who was slain at the Battle of Moytura.

Yet of all these stones, it is those in the walls of the fields that
impress one most. Looking out over this intricate maze of little
paddocks one is staggered to think of the centuries of labour
that went into extracting them from the earth, lighting the turf
fires that would crack them, and piling them up, and it is in
this land that the farmers will tell you that the stones *grow* out
of the ground until they come back in the morning to find more
than were ever there before.

That evening as we sat on the pleasant and sunny terrace of
Ashford Castle Hotel and looked down the broad reach of
Corrib among the scattered islands we allowed our imaginations
to carry us forward some twenty or thirty years, to a time when
the same quay would be alive with pleasure boats waiting to lock
up through the Cong Canal. By then there should be adequate
charts to warn yachtsmen of the reefs and shallows, and the
magic of the islands should be available to many.

To the north of the Corrib Navigation lies the countryside
around Sligo made famous by Ireland's greatest English language
poet, William Butler Yeats, and landmarks like Cummen
Strand, the long beach on the Atlantic side of the town, and
Knocknarea, the tall hill to the south-west, are known well to
those who have read his verse.

Lough Gill is a magical lake some four miles long, scattered
with islands, where you can walk down to the shore to see
Yeats' enchanted Isle of Innisfree, or Tree Island, entirely overgrown with oaks; the "bee-loud glade", therefore still exists,
though one wonders where the poet would have found room
to plant his nine bean-rows, and a good deal of stern labour
would have been needed to provide space enough for his small

124

hut. In fact he never settled on an island but bought an old tower-house at Ballylee in County Galway; a place where, as he recounts in his verse, some long-dead knight had gathered around himself a small troop of swordsmen:

> Gathered a score of horse and spent his days
> In this tumultuous spot
> Where through long wars and sudden night-alarms
> His dwindling score and he seemed castaways.

The first poetry to inspire Yeats as a boy was an old volume of songs of the Orange Men of the North which had been thrown away in his grandfather's stables, and he was so excited by this discovery that his parents, who were artists, decided to encourage his talents. His maternal grandfather, William Pollexfen was a shipowner, and captained sailing barques trading out of Sligo, but his grandfather and great-grandfather were Anglican clergymen, and the boy was destined to follow in their footsteps, though a combination of his father's rationalism and the scientific theories of Darwin excluded him for ever from orthodox Christian belief.

Yeats' poetry was inspired by the urge to give Ireland a native literature in English, and he was among the founders of that Celtic Twilight school of poetry which brought to life once again, in an embroidery of old mythologies, the haunting tales of Cuchulain and Aengus, of Maeve and the wandering *sidhe* who peopled the winds which poured in from the Atlantic across the mountains of Donegal and Sligo. The power of his poetry was greatly strengthened by his unrequited love for Maude Gonne. Though her father was an English Colonel she strongly supported the revolutionary cause, and the use of violence to attain self-government. Yet from originally finding that a "terrible beauty" had been born out of the resistance movement Yeats, who had largely helped to inspire it, found himself disillusioned with the continuing violence and wrote, in 1919:

> Many ingenious lovely things are gone . . .
> We pieced our thoughts into philosophy,
> And planned to bring the world under a rule,
> Who are but weasels fighting in a hole.

After the Kaiser's War, aided by Lady Gregory, he founded a national theatre in Dublin which has been of immense and lasting benefit to the nation, but then he turned his back on Irish mythology and wrote considerably more biographical and political work which seldom has such a wide appeal as his earlier poetry. In 1917 he had married an English lady and later he became a Senator in the government of the Free State, and a very competent one. While he was glad that independence had been attained he regretted the passing of the great houses and "the ascendancy" who with all their faults, alone he felt could provide the nation with a cultural continuity.

I already had some inkling of the archaeological theories which were to form the most important discoveries of our voyage, and a fleeting visit to Tara was a vital part of our inquiry. There is little enough to see of the mound which marks the ancient "capital" of Meath, for it is only a large, low hump on the left of the main road from Dublin to Navan, not far from the village of Dunshaughlin, but with a small knowledge of the site it becomes vividly alive.

The King who ruled at Tara was both a man and the living incarnation of a god, and as such he could not, at least up to about the first century A.D., die of old age but was either ritually killed or was carried off by illness, war or accident. He was largely a god of fertility, and while he reigned was expected to control the weather, which must have been a harrowing task in Ireland, and to produce good hunting and fishing as well as bumper crops. He was generally the incarnation of the sun-god, of which the "fire boar" was the animal symbol, and as such he was the source of all warmth and responsible for kindling the ceremonial Samain fire for the surrounding countryside on November 1 and again at Beltine on May 1. Though an 'eternal' fire was kept burning at Tara under the auspices of the ruler-god it may well be that the ceremonial relighting took place at Tlachtga, a hill a few miles away to the north west. In earlier centuries Tara may well have been chosen as the site of the King's palace because, from this tor commanding the hunting-grounds of central Meath the fire of the boar could be seen for many miles around. There may also be some link between this

126

site and the wonderful burial chambers at New Grange on the River Boyne, for the Celts probably adopted some of the religious customs of their Iberian predecessors.

In time the kingship became more hereditary, though it did not always pass to the eldest son, and as the rulers of Tara were only eminent among equals in a loosely-knit political structure they often found themselves at war with the other local kings. So for a long time the O'Neills reigned at Tara, and later the O'Connors. The tall stone of Fal which is still there is surrounded by an iron fence and this rather white-coloured standing-stone seems to have been the centre of the coronation tests undergone by each prospective claimant to the throne, to assess his suitability for the office. It may be more genuine than the stone of Scone which rests upon the throne at Westminster Abbey, and was formerly believed to be the seat on which the Kings of Tara were crowned.

The Assembly Hall, where the banquets were held, was the most important building at Tara, and lay almost due south of the tip of King Cormac's House, the larger of the two mounds which can still be seen on the crest of the hill. Only a few humps of the Assembly Hall can be distinguished now, for unlike so many of the early churches, it was built of wood which crumbled into the turf, but it was a considerable building, and decorated with the finest craftsmanship that the country could produce. The king and his chief ministers dined on couches under façades of bronze embossed with gold mined from the Wicklow Mountains. Above the royal couch glowed carbuncles and precious stones, reflecting the light from glass windows which were introduced into the country soon after the Roman conquest of Britain.

The seating and feasting was arranged with the meticulous care of a modern state banquet. Not only did each courtier have his place allotted according to his vocation and rank but he was also allocated a specific cut of the joint and the animal which was most highly prized was the wild boar. Hunting has always been the favoured pastime of aristocracies, ranging from pig-sticking under the British Raj to the highly ceremonial boar hunt in the beautiful mediaeval poem of *Sir Gawain And The*

Green Knight. It is therefore understandable that the *torc tened* or 'fire boar' sometimes called the *torc caille* or 'forest boar' should have been at the centre of Celtic feasting and worship, and fire and warmth were particularly significant in a rainy climate. The King was also responsible for the ceremonial hunt undertaken *for the sake* of the renewal of the woodlands and the animal life which they supported.

In the feasting which followed the chief poets, who were among the most important courtiers, were given the hog's haunches, and sat near the king and queen. The braziers, the smiths and the goldsmiths also held seats of honour; particularly the smiths, who sat opposite the king, for it was their technological superiority which forged the weapons which destroyed the Iberian power and helped the Irish to conquer what is now Western Scotland, but the Druids and soothsayers were encouched a little away from the royal dais, which clearly did not permit theology to encroach too nearly on its divine right of kings. Each man's blazoned shield hung above his place, and the long hall was lit by fires, candelabra and lanterns. A magic cauldron possibly associated with Cernunnos, the fertility god of the underworld, bubbled in the centre, and Professor Mac-Alister tells us that "there were 14 doors, and the meal was served by 300 cupbearers, 150 cooks, 50 stewards, 50 footmen and 50 guards." The hall was about 700 feet long and was said to be 30 cubits high and built of gigantic beams. Whenever the Celts constructed a new building of this kind the body of a man was buried alive beneath it so that his spirit would enter into it and endow it with his strength, a strikingly unpleasant example of sympathetic magic which MacAlister suggests may even have extended to the construction of the early Christian buildings on Iona.

Several of the ancient main roads of Ireland led to Tara. Significantly, three of them ran to the water highway of the Shannon, one to the navigable Liffey, and one to Emain Macha, a little to the south of Lough Neagh. The great western road, the Slige Mor, passed close to Clonmacnois, crossed the Shannon, and terminated at the foot of the Corrib Navigation, thus linking water transport with the highways.

7a Kay and Hugh Malet watching a sailing race
from the Mary Ann, on Lough Erne.

7b Island fisherman off Horse Island, Lough Erne.

The long decline of Tara began when it ceased to be a religious sanctuary and Christian administrative synods superseded the Druidic rites. Some later chronicler invented a delightfully dramatic story to illustrate the manner in which the theocracy of Tara was crushed at a single blow by St. Patrick.

According to this tale, on the evening of Beltine, March 25 (the Druid's lunar calendar differed from ours) in the year 433, all fires had been extinguished in and around the royal fortress except the sacred flame of the *torc tened*. The king and all his court were waiting as twilight fell for that rekindling which would announce the birth of spring and guarantee the fertility of all created things, when suddenly they saw a small light flickering in the distance, over by the River Boyne : someone had kindled a fire, and the Druids well knew that no one but a Christian could have been so presumptuous. Thus do the chroniclers enshrine the memory of this transition but inevitably there is no genuine record of the contest which followed between Patrick and the Druid seers, for the tale is simply another example of the oral tradition of recording, in a still miraculous fashion, an event which in fact was probably far less dramatic, though there must indeed have been a period of conversion when the fire of the sacrificial forest boar was gradually extinguished from all the High Places of Ireland. Moreover, the latest evidence clearly indicates that there was no *High* King governing at Tara at that time, or any very certain proof that the god-ruler of Meath held any spiritual precedence over the other five or six local chieftains.

Ireland was therefore, in pagan times, ruled largely by incarnate local kings, and by priests and poets. For its time the system worked quite well and stamped the national character with a theocratic idealism, a love of beauty and of beautiful workmanship, a remarkable oral tradition and perhaps a touch of impracticality which persists. This all evolved, not from a pastoral, but from a hunting society, and it may not be a coincidence that John Kennedy, an Irish American President, gathered poets and men of learning around his hall in Washington. Tara remained the seat of Kings, but Christian synods succeeded the pagan assemblies, and it ceased to be politically important after 1100, except when Daniel O'Connell held the greatest of his gatherings there during his struggle for Home Rule from 1840–43.

A few miles from Tara lies the River Boyne Navigation which once knew the coracles of the pre-Celtic peoples who built along its banks the early burial chambers of Newgrange, Dowth and Knowth, carved with concentric whorls which may well be linked as symbols of the sun, with the fertility flame of the wild boar at Tara. Now derelict, the Boyne was made fully navigable up to Navan by 1800, and though never a very profitable venture it offered a useful service to the surrounding country for some sixty-five years. It is not as simple a matter as some have suggested to assess the precise profitability of a method of transport. Roads seldom bring exact financial returns, but some of their users have to pay for their construction and maintenance by buying licences. Canals were generally maintained by charging tolls, though they were often generously subsidized in Ireland to encourage the growth of industry. James McCann, the greatest director of the Grand Canal Company took over the Boyne believing that a further extension inland would make it pay better and he may have aimed at linking up with Lough Ramor to open all the central plain of Meath to water transport, but his early death was a sad loss to the cause of inland navigation in Ireland and his plans were never fulfilled.

Some two miles west of Drogheda stands the 150 foot high obelisk which commemorates the Battle of the Boyne, where William III, the Dutch Prince of Orange, with an army of some 35,000 defeated James II, who commanded a mixed force of some 25,000 French and Irish, on July 1, 1690. James travelled south from Dublin and the last place at which he trod the soil of his former kingdom was, according to local tradition, the abandoned quay opposite Little Island, downriver from Waterford, where we had fitted out the *Mary Ann* at the beginning of our voyage.

Returning to Jamestown we drove up the Shannon to look at Lough Allen which was once linked to the rest of the navigation, though the two essential locks are now disused. Even in 1896 when Harvey wrote of this four mile long cut he complained that it was in disrepair. Of the nearby village of Drumshambo he wrote: "Previous to 1825 it was a wretched hamlet, desperately dependent for support on illicit distillation."

Lough Allen is a fine open stretch some 8 miles long and 3 miles across, and with its deep water, a magnificent lake for sailing. A small peninsula on the west coast guards the remains of a church associated with St. Patrick, an island off the northern shore contains the ruins of an oratory and close to the east coast lies a crannog of a sept of the O'Reilly, referred to in 1244 in *The Annals of the Four Masters*, when Teige, grandson of Cathal O'Connor of the wine-red hand had his eyes put out and was then hanged "on the festival of St. Berach by Cuconnaught O'Reilly . . . having been kept in confinement by him from the festival of St. Martin till that time." What a charming way to celebrate a holy day! We wondered what St. Martin and Berach thought about these goings-on. A less gruesome mention of this crannog, which can be seen clearly from the nearby road, comes from Harvey, who claimed that a gentleman was building a lodge on it in 1895, but now no trace of it remains.

The Arigna Mountains on the west bank contained coal and iron which has been worked out. Unfortunately these deposits were not sufficient to realize the dream of a prosperous industrial heart for the Irish economy – the coal which the Irish waterways needed so badly "at their heels", as the Duke of Bridgewater would have put it! Some lingering traces of terminals and jetties for carrying by barge can still be seen on the western shore.

Chapter 11

OVER THE BORDER

H ONOR TRACY once claimed that she would be permanently happy in Ireland as long as she was permanently in trouble because the people are so skilled at consoling one. We were in trouble. With a small boat which weighed perhaps half a ton or so and the beautiful Ballinamore and Ballyconnell Canal which once linked the Shannon Navigation to Upper Lough Erne through five highland lakes closed, weeded-up and disintegrating, no water road to Erne remained. We had already travelled more than half-way across Ireland by water, sometimes crossing stretches where there were only a few inches of it, but even our boat could not propel itself over dry land. The Ballinamore is some 38 miles long with sixteen locks, but was never made properly navigable for reasons which will be explained later.

It was Mr. Henry Burke of Ballinamallard who came to our aid and after that we had no more worries, for the powerful machinery of northern efficiency took over entirely. There was not a soul to be seen, not so much as a cat stirring at Carrick-on-Shannon when Mr. Burke, Ernie Irvine and Sam Fiddis drove into the town.

The *Mary Ann* was moored near the ramp, and I ran the boat as high as she would go on to the submerged trailer, where iron clamps were wrapped tightly around her hull. The ramp proved extremely steep, and though the jeep tugged and pulled it could not conquer the gradient. With the aid of Clive Bewley and Sean MacBride, who had been our host on the *Gillaroo* at Jamestown we acquired a tractor from the nearest garage. The tractor towed the jeep, the jeep towed the trailer, the trailer carried the boat, and with the mighty roar of a blast-off they accelerated up the slope amid clouds of exhaust-smoke, and, surrounded by a powerful smell of burnt tyres, shot into the main street of Carrick, nearly colliding with a stray heifer,

132

which had never before encountered any traffic at such an early hour.

Passing the brief formalities of two customs posts at the border we entered the carefully organized world of Enniskillen with its thirty mile an hour signs, Keep Lefts and Halts, which were then almost unknown in the south. My only previous acquaintance with Enniskillen was just after Hitler's war, in Austria, where we encountered a number of quiet men with feathers in their berets, who looked as though they were judiciously estimating the precise point in an anatomy into which a bayonet would sink with the maximum results and the minimum resistance. Though the town has given two regiments to the British army it has, nowadays, no open overtones of war. Its main street curves up and over a steep hill, its vast town hall reflects the continuing prosperity of the shops in its bustling lanes, and its citizens take a justifiable pride in their industry and progressiveness, assessing with a nice precision the collective value of the cars which accumulate there on market days.

The six counties is by no means the Black North, or bogeyland of Southern legend. One's first impression of Fermanagh is of a territory where, in contrast to the South, the country house has managed, albeit rather tenuously, to survive more or less intact. For historical reasons of land tenure, the rackrenting and absenteeism was less severe, and one therefore encounters firmer gradations of society in this area. In one year the government of Northern Ireland managed to create 56,000 new jobs for the entire country, but the birth rate is high, and as 80,000 men were seeking employment a certain amount of emigration remains inevitable. Although the population of Fermanagh in 1961 did not exceed 52,000, those who remain are generally prosperous and cheerful. The silent revolution continues there as elsewhere in Britain, for one tractor and one combine and one milking-machine drive several men off the land to seek employment in industry, but there are not sufficient factories to keep pace with the rapid growth of population, and a man's employment could still depend to some extent on which church he preferred to pray in on Sunday.

At the water customs at Enniskillen we encountered some difficulty since they found it hard to comprehend that a boat could have originally sailed from Ipswich to Waterford by way of Birmingham, Llangollen and Limerick, and seemed uncertain whether she fitted precisely into the category of a seafaring or a landfaring vessel.

We eased the *Mary Ann* into the water at Goblusk Bay, the headquarters of the Lough Erne Yacht Club which was founded in 1820. The splendid gently sloping ramp was one of the few remaining relics of vast seaplane bases built during Hitler's war to fight the Battle of the Atlantic. A flying boat from Lough Erne was one of the first to sight the German warship Bismarck, and in the houses round the lake they still talk of the wonderful party held in the Mess on the night when its crew returned. Sunderlands and Catalinas were based on Erne and were particularly valuable for rescuing the crews of sunken Merchant Navy vessels. Sam Fiddis, who had helped us over the border had been two days in the water when his ship had gone down. On the shoals in the centre of the lake we noticed a few wires clinging to the rocks where the lights of the long runway once guided many a battered flying boat back to base and a warming tot for the crew. At the end of the war the planes were brought out on to the runways and smashed up for scrap; we could still see some of the nuts and bolts embedded in the interstices of the concrete.

Our own boat was only nominally waterproof, for large lumps of tar held in by paint covered a good section of the hull and these had been shaken out by overlanding her, so that we spent a further spell scraping and repairing with paint dripping down into our hair. With the launching ceremony came Mervyn Dane and his television camera, and a formal visit to Devenish Island where further films were taken as we wandered around the ruins looking like crosses between creatures from outer space and dilapidated deep-sea fishermen.

The immense Erne Navigation now lay open to us but there was already the beginning of an autumnal nip in the air so we found it essential to plan and select the main points of interest with care. The River Erne rises in Lough Gowna, County Long-

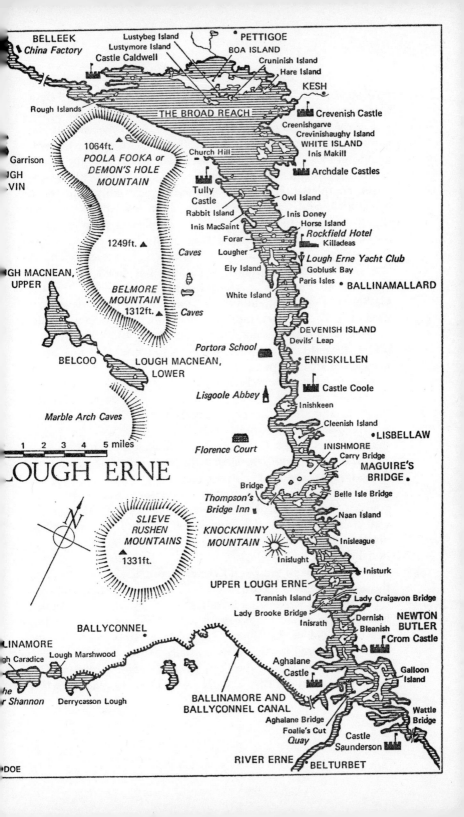

ford, not so far from Lough Ree, and could be navigated by a shallow boat all the way from Lough Oughter to Belleek at the foot of the navigation. It reaches the sea at Ballyshannon, but you cannot take a boat beyond Belleek because, although work was begun on locks to link the lake with the estuary, past the rapids where the hydro-electric stations now stand, this navigation was never completed. The Erne is mostly reasonably safe for a small boat, and has fifty-seven islands in the upper lake and ninety-six in the lower one, though a number of these are mere rocks. At one time the reach between Belturbet and Belleek was the longest navigable waterway in Britain without any lock on it, but this record was broken when the low flood gates were installed at Portora to control the flow available for the Cathaleen Falls dam, though in summer this check is seldom used. The Erne is even more suitable than the Shannon for the smaller sailing and motor boats, and about 1890 was given a 6-foot draught throughout to accommodate the increasing number of steamships.

Although not quite so long as the Shannon, the Erne provides, if possible, an even more fascinating hunting ground for the historian and the archaeologist, with one of the noblest of the early Christian sanctuaries at Devenish and the two vital pagan Celtic centres of the Druids on White Island and on Boa.

It was not without reason that the lower lake was chosen as a flying-boat base during Hitler's war, for the area south of the Broad Reach is free from storms in all but a northerly gale. It is guarded by the peak of Cullen which rises some 900 feet to the west and breaks, if it does not entirely fend off, the prevailing north-westerly wind, while the closely-packed islands offer additional shelter.

One does not go to Lough Erne expecting Riviera weather, for the whole of this seaboard has a high average rainfall, and with the *Mary Ann* swallowing lake-water underneath and collecting rain on top we had to perform a twice daily penance of bailing oily water out of the bilges. The only way to travel in Ireland is to go prepared for the worst possible weather, and then one is pleasantly surprised on the days when it does not happen. Our headquarters on the Erne was the yacht club at Killadeas where we had the advantage of a dry roof over our heads, for the colder autumn nights combined with the heavy rainfall to make camping impracticable. Certainly the ancient gods of these lakes were doing their utmost to guard their secrets from us but we knew where they were lurking and were determined to seek them out.

Chapter 12

DEATH OF THE GODS

WITH the *Mary Ann* patched up but still leaking considerably, we set off one windy morning for Castle Archdale and White Island, and on the way called at Inis MacSaint, where the maintenance men of the navigation were driving in piling for a new landing stage. One of them told me that he had been shipwrecked on a nearby island and had had to remain for two nights before being rescued; when at length they arrived home some of the crew learned that they had been given up as lost at sea and that work had already begun on their coffins. "D'you hear it now?" he asked suddenly, and as I listened I could hear distinctly, but very far away, a faint soughing of wind and water. "Those are the waves breaking on the Broad Reach at the other end of the lake," he said. "I've never been all the way down it myself, but," he added with a glance at the *Mary Ann*, "it can be a treacherous place in a small boat."

The Broad Reach lies at the northern end of Lough Erne, and bearing this timely warning in mind we studied it with care from the Bronze Age tumulus which crowns Inis MacSaint. This tumulus was raided and dug up by amateur grave robbers one night well within living memory and I was told that golden ornaments were discovered which were melted down and sold. As we stood there with the shreds of mist sailing in from the Atlantic we almost fancied that the angry spirit of that vanished warrior king was a tangible reality. The sea never seems far away on the lower lake, for the tang of it comes drifting in on the prevailing wind.

The name Inis MacSaint has no connection with monasticism but means the Island of Sorrel, a wild herb of several varieties, all very much akin to spinach, which was once highly prized as a vegetable addition to the diet. Now that we have become cultivators we have almost lost the art of collecting edible wild herbs with the possible exception of blackberries, mushrooms and cress, but the Iberians and the Celts knew quite literally how to live off the land, and indeed they had to know because game grew steadily scarcer as the population increased and many of their cattle had to be killed off in winter for lack of feed. The monks were seldom hunters, though they were keen fishermen, and so they prized the areas where sorrel grew wild – the rather damp uplands of this island being sufficiently prolific to merit a specific name. Wild sorrel still formed part of the Irish countryman's diet down to the late eighteenth century.

St. Nened studied under St. Finnian of Clonard, "the doctor of wisdom, and tutor of the saints of Ireland in his time", at Moville, near the head of Strangford Lough in County Down, and his fellow students are said to have included Ciaran, Molaise and Maedoc. He founded his abbey on this island about the year 530. St. Ciaran of Clonmacnois not only lent him a book, but also made a voyage to Inis MacSaint to visit his fellow student in 534. Nened's bronze bell, which was preserved in the chapel until it fell into disuse, can now be seen at the National Museum of Scotland in Edinburgh.

We stepped down from the hilltop just as the sun shone out on the little oratory and the magnificent unadorned cross which stands beside it. The cross was raised about the end of the eighth century, and is far the largest that I have seen in Ireland, the vast base being hewn from a single stone which must weigh several tons, while the rest, soaring to 14 feet above one's head is very gently curved on the Maltese pattern. Though it was covered for some way up with the scribblings of vandals, we were amused by the practical humour of the Ministry of Works, which had provided a blank board bearing the simple legend *Record Your Visit Here.* Judging by the number of names on it, it had drawn a good deal of fire from the ancient monuments around. There is a tradition that every Easter dawn, if you should happen to be awake on Inis MacSaint, you will hear the cock crow thrice and the great cross turns full circle on its base at each cry. Legends of this kind are usually based on reality, and it may well be that a relic of St. Peter is associated with the island. The magnificent bronze Lough Erne Shrine, now in the National Museum, Dublin, was dredged up by some fishermen about 1890 off the north point of this island, where it was probably dropped during a Viking raid. These shrines were cases of elaborately carved metalwork – many of silver or gold – and often encrusted with jewels, and were either designed for carrying relics or as safe covers for the illuminated psalms and gospels.

Owl Island lies a little farther north and was we thought, far the most beautiful of all the many islands that we had seen. The carefully cultivated fields stretched up and over the hill and the harbour was neat and trim in the centre of the gently curving bay, with an excellent quay and a buoy for mooring the larger boats. The two Ternan brothers lived there with their father; Douglas Ternan built boats but their main livelihood came from eel-fishing. Their house, set back a little from the bay was glistening with a new coat of whitewash, while an orchard and a half field of potatoes stretched behind it, the runnels cut deep to carry the water away. In their house were wooden platters polished by perhaps 300 years of use, but now pensioned off into the honourable retirement of ornamenting the dresser. They told us of the long, hard winter of 1947 when they had ridden bicycles across the frozen lake to the mainland and back again, of setting the lines for eel-fishing and of the maddening *cutters* which they thought might be mayfly grubs though they held that there was another water insect which was also guilty. These *cutters* cling to the long line set to catch the eels, and if the thread is at all old will bite right through it, destroying many hours of patient work, but they only begin to wreak their havoc in the late summer and autumn and the islanders have learned to set their lines at cunning angles to decrease their depredations.

As we emerged from the cover of Rabbit Island we encountered the full blast of the waves of the Broad Reach whipped on by the prevailing wind and sometimes breaking on the crests. To reach White Island we had to steer diagonally across this barrage and the critical moments came when we reached the top of the breakers. Soon Kay was bailing frantically to keep us afloat, while every now and again a gallon or two of water would lap over the gunwale. How often must the saints who voyaged in cots and coraghs have found themselves in a similar plight and sought their comfort in the Psalm:

Save me, O God
For the waters have risen to my neck.
I have sunk into the mud of the deep and there is no
*   foothold.*
I have entered the waters of the deep and the waters
*overwhelm me.**

We would have kept much drier if we had set the bow into the waves as we had done on Lough Ree, but we were anxious to avoid the heart of the Broad Reach that day in case the storm increased.

The breakers certainly towered above us but there was nothing as complicated as the box waves which we had met on the Shannon. We rocked and rolled over the white-capped crests until we ran under the sheltering headland opposite Inchmakill, and on to the still waters of Castle Archdale Bay with its magnificent quays built for flying boats, and the ships riding at anchor.

John Archdale and his family came from Darsham Hall in Norfolk and for the sum of £5 6s. 8d. they obtained, at the beginning of the Plantation period about 1610, a thousand acres of arable land around their tower house. The old castle stands up the hill in the forestry plantation and is worth a visit. There are the remains of a T-shaped house and a square tower in which the pear-shaped gun ports are rather unusual. A panel over the door records 1615 as the date of completion, and the family motto. The castle was captured by Rory Maguire in 1641, though the heir was saved by the nurse, but it was burned again in 1689 and a new and larger building constructed nearby. The Archdales are the last of the original settler families on Lough Erne to survive.

Castles are a most important feature of the Irish landscape and you will find them every few miles, for life was so insecure and struggles among the various clans and factions so much an accepted part of everyday existence that it was generally unsafe

Psalm 68. Gelinot Version.

to live outside one. The lakes and rivers make an especially happy hunting ground for these forts because they were mostly built where there was an adequate water supply and where stone and timber could be carried in large quantities on rafts or barges. Many of the castles within the Pale were constructed after the Act of 1429 which offered a subsidy of ten pounds to those who would build to government specifications: a remaining example is Donore on the River Boyne. We have two vivid portraits of life in these tower houses from visitors of the seventeenth century. M. Le Gouz, a Frenchman, wrote:

> The castles of the nobility consist of four walls; extremely high and thatched with straw; but to tell the truth they are nothing but square towers; or at least having such small apertures as to give no more light than there is in a prison. They have little furniture, and cover their rooms with rushes, of which they make their beds in summer, and straw in winter. They put their rushes a foot deep on their floors and on their windows, and many of them ornament their ceilings with branches.

Luke Gernon, an Englishman, produced a racy description about 1620 praising the hospitality more highly than the cuisine:

> The castles are built very strong and with narrow stayres for security. The hall is the uppermost room, let us go up, you shall not come down agayne till tomorrow. . . . The lady of the house meets you with her trayne . . . salutations past, you shall be presented with all the drinkes in the house, first the ordinary beer, then aqua vitae, then sacke, then old ale, the lady tastes it, you must not refuse it. The fyre is prepared in the middle of the hall, where you may solace yourself till supper time, you shall not want sacke or tobacco. By this time the table is spread and plentifully furnished with variety of meates, but ill-cooked and without sauce. . . . When you come to your chamber do not expect canopy and curtaines. . . .

Nor would the visitor of that time have expected very much in the way of chairs. A few benches and settles made up largely

142

from strong-boxes might have been scattered around the hall but up to about 1600, to eat their meals they still reclined like the Romans on couches, the food being placed on low tables on their left-hand side. The plantation castles were a little more advanced in their fittings and equipment, but the difference was not considerable.

On Davy's Island, in Archdale Bay, a number of foreign medieval coins have been discovered which suggest that there was once a hostel there for pilgrims travelling along the Way of the Saints to visit some of the many local shrines. Similar hostels have been traced on the Upper Lake at Galloon, and on Cleenish Island, where the landlady was Joan Maguire, her guests arriving in the rather cramped dug-out canoes, and going on to visit the shrines and abbeys *en route* to the main pilgrimage at little Lough Derg.

There was a useful jetty to moor to on White Island and we soon found the grey stone chapel with its carved figures set into the north wall and the roof open to the sky. From the crown of this island radiate the mysterious earthworks of a sanctuary which has never yet been excavated. The sculptures represented to some extent the grail of our voyage, for we had travelled over hundreds of miles of lakes and had sought out innumerable misty islands in the hope of bringing to life once again some of the people who had lived and loved, worshipped, fought and cast their spells in the days when these lakes were densely populated. Man was wont to create his gods largely in his own image, so the sculptor's hand had placed them before us on the wall of this Chapel, with their broad Irish faces, and the stone seemed to glow into life with the knowledge which we had so painstakingly garnered along the Way of the Saints.

On the extreme left is a strangely cross-legged female fertility figure like a lady leprechaun; indeed the very word *luchurpan*, meaning *little body* seems to fit her precisely, and she is wearing a brimless hat and grinning with diabolical delight. Crude and vital, puckish and irascible, she represents a belief far older than the Druids that all fertility in man and woman, beast and plant and tree springs from such demanding local godlets who had to be propitiated; yet her very vitality prevents

143

her from seeming as deeply evil as the Janus gods of Boa which we encountered later. In early times such figures were carved from wood and were adopted by the Druids for worship in their sanctuaries, and oak groves, stunted by the Atlantic winds still flourish on these islands. Later they were sculptured in stone and even incorporated into churches just in case they might still be spiritually useful; gargoyles are indirect descendants of these *sheelnagigs*, as the Irish call them, and the Lady Chapel of Mere Church in Wiltshire has an interesting example of a fertility god in its roof. These little elfin deities had to be served by human sacrifice which was later commuted to animal sacrifice, otherwise they would not provide for the pressing needs of harvest and of hunting, and one Roman author, Lucan, has left us a harrowing description of a Druid grove in France, with the idols and branches smeared with human blood. It is quite possible that this figure is Morrigu, the great queen, and supreme war goddess of the Gaels, who would manifest herself in battle as a lean, grey-haired hag, shrieking and screaming and hopping over the points of the swords and spears and shields and inspiring the warriors to clinch the victory. She sometimes took the form of a hooded crow and it was she who settled on Cuchulain's head as he bled to death.

Next to this little devil is an unknown god who is dressed in such a fine tunic that he fits in well with that dandified deity Elathan, the beautiful and evil prince of darkness, who is described as wearing a shirt interwoven with threads of gold, and covered with a mantle of gold braid, while his hands vanish into a small oblong muff; some have claimed him as a gospel bearer of the Christian era, but his clothes look rather too fine for one espoused to poverty.

Nowhere will you see better the transition from paganism to Christianity than in this wonderful array of early sculptures, for the next character represents the faith which, with its message of love, hope and charity banishes the satanic forces of the Celtic pantheon. This is the Presbyter Abbot with his cowl which the Druid poets satirized, his pastoral shepherd's staff for herding the foolish and straying flock towards salvation, and the small bell which summons them to worship the Nazarene.

9a The Lugnath Stone
on Inchagoill Island,
Lough Corrib.

9b Female fertility figure –
probably the
Morrigu – White Island.

10a
The author fishing on
Inchagoill Island, Corrib.

10b
A typical Irish coragh –
Aran Islands.

He may be a bishop but, strangely to us, bishops were often less important in the Celtic Church than abbots, and therefore less likely to be worthy of portraiture. As a young man this abbot would have sailed his coragh to tht remotest islands of the Way of the Saints, and helped to build his church and found his monastery; indeed, this could be the greatest of the Bishops, St. Patrick himself.

Next comes an ancient pagan god of music represented by an Irish piper with his bagpipe tucked under his arm and the chanter held out in front. His facial muscles seem strained with the effort and his eyes have the fixed stare of concentration. He could be Angus, the Gaelic Eros, who is associated with music, but he was generally an exponent of the harp rather than of the pipes, so that this is more probably a less important god who happens to have survived by sheer good fortune.

Next to him comes the most fascinating character of all, Manannan Mac Lir, the special patron of sailors, and son-god of that old master of the waters who is reputedly buried on the coast of Lough Corrib. Manannan was one of the best loved and one of the last to survive among the Celtic pantheon, until St. Brendan took his place. Emhain of the Apple Trees, an island in the Firth of Clyde was one of his headquarters, another his native Isle of Man, but he roamed abroad in his boat called the *Wavesweeper* which needed no helm or oars, for it guided and propelled itself at its master's whim. His great horse, *Splendidmane* sped faster than the wind, and a blow from his sword, *The Retaliator* could not fail to slay. It was he, the god of the waters who kept the magic boars on his islands to feed the other gods, but they were never consumed without renewing themselves entirely. It was he, the master of the waves, who provided the *Feast of Age*, that wonderful and mysterious pork banquet of the gods and those who ate of it could never grow old. There he stands engaged in the very ancient religious ritual of confronting two animals to prove, perhaps, the power of man over the lesser creatures of creation, and the animals which he holds are young hogs, or boars. This statue is a very crude and primitive example of the fine stone carving from Euffigneix in Haute Marne, France, called The God of Euffigneix, on which the boar is shown far more distinctly carved but with the head straight; the similarity of line and the absolute clarity of the cloven hoofs on both sculptures exclude any doubt. The mark of the boar has been found at several sites in Scotland, and Professor Powell tells us that the boar was the "most conspicuous emblem" of the Celts in France during the last phase of their independence, while its spirit was also at the centre of the feasting and 'eternal' flame which burned at Tara.

The clues mount up, for if you travel about three miles south of Inverness railway station, in that part of Scotland once conquered by the Irish, you will find an ancient slate with a carving of the Celtic fire boar on it, and above his head is the sun with its rays shining down on to the hackles on his back; the stone stands in a field near the road at Knocknagael, which means the hill of the Gaels. Thus nature, man and beast meet in a fascinating trinity at the heart of the ancient Celtic faith. Nature was represented by a strange dualism of beasts and vegetables, the fish and the bulrush being the symbols of Manannan who, though he provided the sacred hogs for the gods did not I believe have them as his familiars. The thorn, so centrally sacred in Ireland and at Glastonbury too must have been the vegetable symbol of Cenn Cruaich, while his animal familiar would have been the wild boar of the Tara sacrifices. The second part of the Trinity was man represented by the incarnate kings and Druids while the third section was pure spirit, the Tuatha de Danaan or warrior gods and goddesses who were not often seen by mortals and were later to be transformed into the elves and fairies of folklore.

Among the vital gods of the Celtic pantheon were Cenn Cruaich who brought all heat, growth, light and hope and especially fires to warm and cook and fashion weapons, and the brooding Cernunnos from whom sprang all fertility in trees and plants and living creatures. His vegetable symbol was corn while his animal familiar was the deer, and that serpent which St. Patrick expunged from Ireland. Man is represented by the local King who was the living incarnation of Cenn and therefore responsible for performing the fertility sacrifices, probably not only at Tara but in all the local ceremonies. The fierce symbol of the sun in the animal kingdom was the wild boar, the creature which, as the *torc triath* or royal swine of Ireland, and the *twrc trwyth* of Welsh mythology had to be ritually sacrificed back to the sun on the high tor of Tara and other sanctuaries (perhaps at Knocknagael and Glastonbury too) in the white hot flames of Samain, to ensure that warmth and light and growth and happiness would return again to gladden the hearts of men. Doubtless in far-off White Island those who could not attend the great Assembly in the 'cathedral' of Tara would perform their own ceremonies before just such a figure as this, with his wide-open eyes fixed in the trance-like gaze of religious transcendentalism. There is a marked similarity between the White Island figures and the thirteen stone statues which once stood in Cenn's sanctuary at Magh Slecht on the portage lakes between the rivers.

Indeed, one heraldic symbol of Ulster might well be the black boar, for he rampages through that kingdom's history like a thing possessed. The Black Pig's Dyke, built about 200 A.D. runs like an earthen Hadrian's Wall along the border of ancient Ulster and was constructed to stop cattle raiding. Only some segments of it remain, for its builders used such natural barriers as forests, bogs and lakes to save digging, but it started on the west coast below Lough Melvin, ran from Lough Macnean to Lough Allen, and from below Lough Allen through Lough Caradice on the approximate route of the Ballinamore Canal close to Magh Slecht, to Lough Oughter. From there it continued across country to Newry. Eventually it suffered the fate of most 'impregnable' fortresses, and was breached by the chieftains called the three Collas, who were ancestors of the Maguires, about 340 A.D. The black boar holds his place yet in Irish superstition, and you could scarcely meet anything more unlucky at night in a lonely place than a dark-coloured pig. Professor J. B. Ruane describes the hogs which grunted and scavenged around the islands of the Druids and the saints with a nice precision: "They had all the characteristics of the wild pig, namely heavy shoulders, light hams, short body, and an ugly head with long tusks:" they were therefore dangerous, and it is not surprising that it was unlucky to meet them in a lonely place after dark. The boars on White Island fit in neatly with

147

this description, with the exception of their curious beak-like mouths, but it must be remembered that these would hang open on a dead animal, a characteristic which the sculptor may have sought to capture.

The last figure in the line is Niet or Nuad, the god of war and the Zeus of the Celtic pantheon, bearing his shield in one hand, and his invincible sword in the other. He had much of Mars in his character, for he delighted and exulted in war, and Charles Squire wrote: "there is little doubt that he was one of the most important gods of both the Gaels and the Britons, for his name is spread over the whole of the British Isles, which we may surmise the Celts conquered under his auspices." It is possible that this figure incorporates some of the identity of Niall of the Nine Hostages, a semi-legendary King of Tara in the fourth century who raided the coasts of Britain and was reputedly slain near Southampton, for men were gods, and gods were seen very much in the image of man. Niet thirsted for blood, and to him the easy swordsmen of Ulster would pay their duty of sacrifice before they went raiding across the border, for they believed that the demands of Niet could be averted from themselves if another victim was sacrificed, and before him they would slay some of their prisoners if they returned in safety.

There remains the mystery of the life of the sculptor himself. The puckish little *sheelnagig* may have been carved by a different hand but the other figures, crude and simple though they are when compared with the technical inspiration of the French Celts who were influenced by Rome, seem to have so many similarities that they must be the work of the same sculptor. Some were found built into the masonry of the church while others were discovered where the conquering faith had toppled them many centuries before. Even allowing for most religious sculpture being formalized, the evidence points towards a single master-craftsman who compensated for his earlier 'errors' by doing a portrait of the local abbot, or perhaps of St. Patrick. There remains the fascinating alternative that one of the early saints, perhaps a missionary of pre-Patrician days from Whithorn Abbey in Wigtownshire showed such admirable qualities that he was accepted into the Druid pantheon.

There are three other important sculptured stones in the cemetery of Killadeas churchyard on the Kesh road, seven miles north of Enniskillen. The famous Bishop's stone of about the seventh or eighth century depicts a little bustling, hunched figure of an abbot with his pastoral walking stick in his hand and a small bell with the clapper hanging out under it; he personifies what later came to be called the muscular school of Christianity. This may well have been an adapted pagan stone, for on the other side is an interlaced pattern and the face of a Druid deity which bears a slight resemblance to the sun. There is also a bullen stone with a cross and traces of an inscription in Gaelic on it, and yet another stone resembling a cross in a boat or ark which has since become the symbol of the modern ecumenical movement, and is clearly eastern in inspiration.

The storm died away as we left White Island and the vast expanse of the Broad Reach lay innocently quiet and placid under the early stars. The gods, it seemed, were no longer determined to foil us now that we had reached their ancient sanctuary. The thin crescent of a Druid moon floated up into the eastern sky and the churning wake of the *Mary Ann* glittered astern as we returned across the Bay to our headquarters at Goblusk.

Chapter 13

THE WITCH GOD

THE Broad reach should be approached with caution by those who set out in small boats and we waited for fine weather since we were growing weary and careless, and it is under such conditions that boating accidents happen. A low ridge of mist hung only a few feet over the lake, but it was lifting gradually and from a point near Rabbit Island we caught a glimpse of the magnificence of Tully Castle, mantled in ivy and standing guard over the western shore. There is good deep water in the centre of Castle Bay, and Tully is worth visiting as a solid example of the plantation castle, built like Crom, Portora, and Belleek, close to the water, which was then the safest and most strategic means of communication. The Protestant settlers first moved into this part of Ireland early in the reign of James I, about 1608, and this conquest of a mainly Roman Catholic population was bolstered by arms for a long time. The Irish clans resisted courageously, but much hatred was bred from the conflict, and a resentment which was formerly beginning to wane as the ecumenical movement stretched its healing hands even into County Fermanagh. Tully surrendered on terms to the resistance movement under Rory Maguire on Christmas Eve 1641, some of its defenders were put to the sword and the building was burned, after which there seems to be no further record of its occupation, though there remain some farm buildings around it.

Beyond Heron Island the huge expanse of the Broad Reach stretched out, seemingly endless as the mist closed down on the far horizon, leaving us immured in an emptiness of cloud and water without a trace of land. Gradually a faint outline of the Poola Fooka, or Demon's Hole Mountains loomed up from the water's edge, while on our right the bed of the lake, carved out by the slow architecture of glaciers dropped away to its deepest point at 208 feet. The water was perfectly still until a

150

sudden breeze from the east swept the mist along the flank of Magho Mountain to shreds, leaving a lacework of white along the fells, and thin veils of cloud here and there towards the summit. The transformation was swift and startling; one moment our world was confined entirely to the lake and the next a towering range of mountains lay revealed as though a dramatic curtain had been raised. There was something Wagnerian in this sudden revelation and one felt that figures more than life-sized might emerge from the boulders on the high fell, and that gnarled and knotted creatures must be entombed in the inner fastnesses of the rock. It would surely have been the range of the Demon's Hole which inspired Allingham's best-known poem, and one which has found its way into so many anthologies:

> *Up the airy mountain,*
> *Down the rushy glen,*
> *We daren't go a-hunting*
> *For fear of little men . . .*

William Allingham lived from 1824–89 and his statue stands beside the road at Ballyshannon in County Donegal. His father was an English bank manager who settled there in Victorian days, and William found his first important employment as supervisor of the customs department when Ballyshannon was a thriving port for sailing vessels and provided shelter on the north Atlantic trade route. Later he moved in this service to London, but turned to writing, and succeeded Froude as editor of Frazer's Magazine. He married Helen Patterson, an artist who made a name for herself as an illustrator and painter in water-colours. Allingham produced several books and plays, but his most lasting achievement was his straightforward but charming lyrical poetry, which shows a considerable technical mastery, and though most of his best work was written in London, the lakes and islands of Fermanagh flow through it like a silver thread of nostalgia:

> *If ever I'm a money'd man, I mean, please God to cast*
> *My golden anchor in the place where youthful years*
> *   were past;*

Though heads that now are black and brown must
*   meanwhile gather grey,*
New faces rise by every breath, and old ones drop away —
Yet dearer still that Irish hill than all the world beside;
It's home sweet home where'er I roam, through lands and
*   waters wide;*
And if the Lord allows me, I surely will return
To my native Belashanny and the winding Banks of Erne!

The sea, for lake is an inadequate term for the Broad Reach, gradually narrowed towards the bird sanctuary of the Rough Islands where we found deep water close in to the south west shore of the largest island. We could discover nothing of the history of this remote archipelago, but as we ate by the water's edge we could hear, though not see, innumerable birds singing in the matted undergrowth around us, for it is preserved as a sanctuary. Beyond the islands we sighted the markers showing the navigable passage; you may pass either side of the diamond-shaped ones but as they often give warning of a large shoal it is wise to give them a sensible berth. Going downstream from Enniskillen to Belleek the markers with the flat tops should be left on the right, or starboard side, and those with a curved head to port, but as there is almost always a cormorant, or a large, fat and pensive seagull meditating on top of them and obscuring the shape, a pair of field glasses can be useful, though they are not essential. We passed beyond Muckinish, or Pig Island, and ran aground off Roscor while trying to avoid a salmon net. Even in the smallest boat it is an alarming experience to be suddenly prised out of the water by a hidden reef, and the seams of the *Mary Ann* opened further, adding to our daily penance of bailing. I suspect that silting has reduced the proper draught of six feet a good deal at this point, and larger craft would be wise to approach it cautiously until it has been dredged again, except in the winter when the lake level is slightly higher.

We were now back between the banks of the river and, aided by a current of some three knots swept under a broad road bridge and on past green fields until we reached White Island at Belleek, where we found a good depth of water up to the stone jetty of the old steamer berth.

The first steamboat to ply was the *Countess of Erne*, a wooden ship with paddles, and though she ran aground near Lisnaskea on her maiden voyage, she served the lakes well for seventeen years. *The Countess of Milan*, named after Lady Caldwell and built at her home on the lower lake sailed for about four years, but her draught prevented her from reaching Enniskillen in dry weather, which was a trading disadvantage. The largest steamer on this navigation was the *Devenish* which plied for some seven years every day in the summer and three times a week in winter, and called anywhere along the lake by request as long as the weather was suitable. She was a fine paddle steamer with a tall rakish funnel and portholes set low in the hull.

John Porter of Belle Isle, on the upper lake, was the greatest inland waterway enthusiast that the Erne has known, and was a Director of the Lough Erne Steamboat Company. He bought the SS *Knockninny* in Dublin and took her along the Grand Canal, up the Shannon and through the vital Ballinamore Canal in 1868, and under Captain Lingard she did good service on the lakes until 1900. Another ship in "Porter's private navy", as it was sometimes called, was the *Belturbet*, a comfortable little steamer with a long cabin and glass windows which ran a market service on the upper lake and carried excursion parties during the summer. Major d'Arcy Irvine, another waterway enthusiast, bought the *Rossclare* in 1866 and used her for a few years as a trading vessel. She was later re-named *The Lady of the Lake*, ran a popular excursion to Castle Caldwell, and was not broken up until 1956. Among the larger sailing ships were the *Martha* and the *Ranger*, both of 30 tons, and the *Royal George* of 10 tons, and there were a number of privately owned steam yachts, so that the lake was an extremely busy navigation in those days. The sole successor of this noble line of ships is Mr. G. McQuillan's *Endeavour* which we had passed off Inis Doney that morning; a clinker-built diesel vessel about 50 feet long which runs excursions from Enniskillen where she was built by her owner, and she has a cruising speed of about eight knots. While the passenger trade and private yachts thrived on the

Erne the carrying trade was not so successful as that of Corrib, the reason being that there was no navigation to link the sea at Ballyshannon with the lakes. Goods could not be loaded over the sides of ships into the lake steamers as they had been at Galway, and so the navigation did not thrive on trade. Nowadays, when all the emphasis is on the passenger service and cabin cruisers, the Erne will certainly come back into its own again, but a very fast service for goods could be provided by hovercraft. This navigation has long outlived the railways which once put it out of business.

After mooring we peered cautiously over the top of the fence, wondering which side of the border we were on, for part of Belleek is in the Republic, and when we went to buy petrol we were told at the filling station that we had strolled over the frontier. "If I want to get into Belleek by car," said the proprietor, "I can't use this road, but have to drive half a mile to the nearest approved one and queue up to get through the customs gate, and the same aggravating process coming back!" We called in at the customs office and asked what would happen if we crossed the border by water and were told that the waterguard was at Enniskillen and only land customs was dealt with at Belleek.

Opposite our quay lay the long classical building where the exquisitely delicate and carefully ornamented Belleek china is manufactured. The complicated and entwining patterns suggest that something of the skill of the early Irish illuminators and metalworkers survives in this pleasant little border town, and this was an ideal place for a pottery since there were supplies of raw materials which have since been worked out on the nearby Castle Caldwell estate; when the factory was founded in 1857 the head of water from the lake drove the machinery. We were told that this water power still turned the turbines which provide the electricity for the factory and the town. As we watched the craftsmen moulding the delicate designs of this handmade china we learned that some of the patterns they use are borrowed and adapted from the Book of Kells, and there is a large export market for it in the English-speaking world, which helps to keep some 120 people employed.

154

Though the weather held fine, returning up river against the current was a slower business and the navigation past Rossmore Point into Bleana Lung Bay calls for care. There are still people in Fermanagh who remember the delightful excursion on the *Lady of the Lake* from Enniskillen to Castle Caldwell, where the passengers walked up to the station and caught a train of the Enniskillen and Bundoran Railway back to town again, but this single track line has been removed, leaving here and there only an occasional deserted station, a viaduct, or a long curving embankment.

Castle Caldwell is tucked well away from winds and storms at the west end of the bay and there is deep water to within some six feet of the old quay which has partly collapsed, and is densely overgrown with trees. The Caldwells were wealthy Enniskillen merchants who bought the tower-house about 1662 and later added an attractive Gothic mansion to the side of it. Like the Archdales, Humes and other landowners around the Erne they lived in almost princely splendour and had the good sense to travel by water in their own state barges with flags and pennants flying and bands to provide music to while away their voyages around the lakes. Less elegant boats drew their supplies and landed them at their doors – sugar, spices, wine, foreign fruits, coffee and tea and all those luxuries which could not be carried to their quays from their local farms came to Ballyshannon by ship, and up from Belleek by barge. That overgrown quay, once such a bustling centre of activity, clearly showed how the water level of the lakes had been dropped artificially some seven or eight feet.

As we walked up the path towards the castle, it led into a hollow, echoing cave, which we entered rather gingerly, for the floor was scattered with boulders which had tumbled from the barrel-vaulted roof. Large beads of water dripped down on us and with unerring aim found the precise gap between my collar and the nape of my neck. At the far end a glimmer of light showed where a curving stone staircase led up from the dungeon to the central hall of the castle, now completely roofless and naked to the sky, though the main walls still stand gauntly around it. It was to this underground chamber that the casks and crates which fed the life of this vast establishment were brought and stored, and it was by this route that Arthur Young, the travel writer would have left his host, Sir James Caldwell after his visit in 1776. He described the picturesque view from the battlements as "the most pleasing that I have anywhere seen", and embarked in the family barge for Enniskillen rowed by six sturdy oarsmen, with the band playing and colours flying.

Only six years before Young's visit one of the fiddlers of this nautical band had taken a dram over the eight, and if drinking and driving is a grave error today, drinking and sailing was as dangerous then, for he slipped, fell overboard and was drowned. Sir James Caldwell, moved by a combination of sorrow, humour and didacticism had a large stone memorial tablet shaped like a fiddle carved in his memory and placed it by the lakeside; it tells how he fell from the

St. Patrick Barge Belonging
TO
Sir James Caldwell Bart.
AND COUNT OF MILAN
& was drowned off this
point August ye 15
1770

Beware ye fidlers of ye fidlers fate
Nor tempt ye deep least ye repent to late
Ye ever have been deemed to water foes
Then shun ye lake till it with whiskey floes
On firm land only exercise your skill
There you may play and drink your fill

D.D.D.
J.D.

How strange a twist of fate that all the splendour of Castle Caldwell should be remembered now partly because it entertained Arthur Young, and partly because of Sir James' jesting tribute to an accident. Though some people do not consider this epitaph to have been in the best of taste, it is possible that the merry fiddler himself would have appreciated it.

Beyond Castle Caldwell, and on the northern side of the

Broad Reach lies the largest inland island in the British Isles, though this rather depends on how you define an island; strictly speaking Boa can no longer claim this record because it is joined to the mainland by bridges at either end, and from our increasing knowledge we speculated that Inchmore on Lough Ree, or Inisleague on the upper lake might now be the runners-up for the title. Boa Island is $4\frac{3}{4}$ miles long and slightly less than a mile across at the widest point. Until the road was built about 1930, this was one of the largest isolated communities in Ireland, and retained an agnatic system of land tenure of which there are still some traces today. We discovered Boa's two greatest treasures lurking by the southern shore behind Round Island; they were in their proper setting, with oak trees branching overhead and nettles sprouting around them. They are two stone statues, each bearing two faces growing out of single necks. The site is also a Christian graveyard which may well date from before St. Patrick's time, for there is an insistent local tradition that this was the second oldest dedicated burial place in Ireland; it is still in use, and was clearly a pagan sanctuary time out of mind before that.

The Janus-gods of Boa are among the earliest standing stone figures surviving in the British Isles. Though the people who carved them would hardly have known it, this god was Etruscan in origin, for the Celts were driven south from their traditional hunting grounds in Austria and Switzerland and conquered the waning Etruscan empire about 400 B.C., assimilating much of its art and religion. Janus is a god of fertility, for primitive peoples associated its duality with the birth of twins as the divine manifestation of the gift of reproduction; there remain in Ireland and on the Continent a few surviving statues with three or even four faces. Originally the Boa gods may have been up to seven feet tall like the similar one at Holzgerlingen in Germany, for though they now stand only some three feet from the ground, there is a clear break in the waist of the larger figure.

I was able to discover a good deal about this Janus god, for the Romans also borrowed him from Etruria. Janus and Jana represent, in their double effigy, the prototype of the joining of man and woman, and it may be that our marriage service owes

157

something to this idea when it says that they shall be one flesh. Thus one half of the sculpture is male and the other is female and they combine to make the god of the very beginning – of creation itself, and of life and fertility – the spirit of opening. Thus by a logical, if curious progression Janus became the classical god of doorways and gates. He was the deity of birth and of all initiation and so the dawn was sacred to him, and to him we are indebted for our word January, marking the beginning or opening of the year. Originally Janus preceded Jupiter, and though later the Romans went after strange gods, Janus retained his ceremonial precedence over the president of the immortals – indeed, Jupiter or Jove is little more than a cognomen for him. As Ivar Lessner has so clearly shown, men really originally worshipped one main god, but later the lesser deities crept in. On the *early* Roman coins Janus is shown as *bearded*, and the Lough Erne god is also clearly bearded, proving the immense antiquity of the idea, if not of the actual carving. It seems, therefore, that the Janus cult was not borrowed from later Roman Britain or from France, but was carried over to Ireland with the earliest waves of Celtic invaders, though inevitably the earlier carvings would have been of wood.

The Celts called Janus Cernunnos, the Horned One, or in Ireland the Dagda, and thought of him as dwelling in or under the earth. They divided their deities into the beneficent powers which brought fertility and the satanic ones which rode the storms and scattered plagues, but with one exception – Manannan Mac Lir – even the best were not very admirable by Christian standards. Cernunnos was therefore technically one of the 'better' spirits and was an oak god; he possessed a magic cauldron and it may well be that the cauldron in the hall at Tara was his, and that he links up in some obscure way with the sacred boar flesh in it. The Celts thought of this god as being immensely potent, powerful and athletic and cut his crude figure of strength and virility some 200-feet tall in the chalk, striding across the downs at Cerne Abbas (note the similar names) swinging a gigantic club which was traditionally made of iron. The hunting representative of Cernunnos in the animal kingdom was the antlered deer, and our morris dancers on Otford Green

158

with the horns on their heads may well be celebrating the folk memory of this vanished deity.

St. Augustine detested Janus and in the City of God, when writing his magnificent diatribe against the old pagan deities, placed him second only in order of repulsiveness to Cybele, the Cretan earth goddess, whose orgiastic rites provided splendid grist for his mill :

> Thus the great mother exceeded all her son-gods, not in greatness of deity, but of obscenity. Janus himself was not as monstrous as this monster. He was but deformed in his statue; but this was both bloody and deformed in her sacrifices. He had members of stone given him, but she takes members of flesh from all her attendance. This shame all Jove's lecheries came short of; he, besides his female rapes, defamed heaven, but with one Ganymede. . . .

It would be difficult to give Cernunnos even so meagre a bill of health as Augustine offered to Janus, for these two figures with their close-set eyes have a ponderous look of evil about them still. The smaller sculpture is called the Lustyman because he was found buried in the monks' churchyard on Lustymore, or Great Fertility Island, just opposite Caldragh, and he should really be returned to his proper site. The male face seems to have been completely erased, possibly because the monks disapproved of its crudity but the female figure bears the vegetable kingdom's symbol of Cernunnos in her hand – a trained botanist might perhaps be able to identify it, but I believe that it is corn.

The largest figure has a libation stoop between the heads, into which the blood of sacrifices would have been poured. The male side of the figure is identified by a phallus and there is a woven pattern in their combined hair. Mrs. Mary Rogers has suggested that the larger figure of Cernunnos may have been a ritual outlier of the nearby stone circle on Boa Island, in which case there could have been a solemn procession to this place of sacrifice, for these figures seem still to be brooding sullenly over memories of the scent of burning flesh. It was curious, but very apposite to find them in the heart of that Christian graveyard at Caldragh, for they show what a long way our theology has carried us. I suspect that the larger Cernunnos owes his survival to having been toppled into the lake by the conquering faith, for a part of Caldragh must have been submerged under the old levels, and lake mud serves as a fine preservative.

Some gods vanish early, others die only very gradually, but Cernunnos is with us still, for he is in origin none other than the central deity of the witches' Sabbat. The original Celtic Cernunnos took the form of a naked giant, the vast warrior deity of the dense woodlands and oak forests, and lord of all the wild beasts which he assembled by striking a stag with his club until its belling brought all the woodland creatures to him. He was the father god, Dagda, Janus or Jupiter of the Celtic nations in whom all the earth's fertility was encompassed, and his iron weapon was, it was said, at least as large as two warriors. His closest familiars were the deer and the snake and in Celtic art he is frequently portrayed grasping a large, ram-headed serpent in his left hand. As the Church took over it found that Cernunnos, or Conall Cernac as he was most probably called in Ireland, was its chief opponent in the struggle for the souls of the people, so it linked him with the snake of the Garden of Eden, and thus the Devil as we know him today was born, with horns and tail already a part of his Druidical equipment, and the hoofs perhaps a later accretion from Thor's sacred goats.

The witches' Sabbat was, I believe, nothing more or less than a continuing worship of this Celtic deity surviving as a declining but rival faith down the centuries, and if we consult Mr. Pennethorne Hughes' scholarly study of witchcraft we can obtain a considerable insight into our ancestral cultic worship.

Before the devotees set out for their gathering they rubbed a carefully prepared grease into their skins compounded of toxic herbs, probably including hemlock, aconite and belladonna, which, aided perhaps by herbal drugs taken internally, would serve to heighten their susceptibilities and even induce hallucinations of flying and leaping. They would gather, perhaps thirteen in all, generally unclothed, around a statue or standing stone like the Lugnath pillar on Inchagoill where a leading Druid masked and horned and clothed in deerhide pre-

11 Manannan (left) and the God of Euffigneix, France,
with attributes of boars which were kept on sacred
islands for the Feast of Age.

12a Turf for the winter in County Donegal.

12b Dinghy racing on Lough Derg, Shannon.

sided over the ceremonies. There was music and singing, and feasting preceded the dancing which probably had a ritual significance; there were congas, weird performances on branches and something similar to jiving, though the ring dance was probably the most popular.

Ritual cannibalism, a frequent facet of the Sabbats, must have derived from the ancient climax of the cult gathering, the eating of the presiding Druid-god himself, but this practice could never have been common, and died out early, the sacrificial substitute being an animal or a baby. Either at or near the end of the ceremony there would be the indiscriminate sexual orgy of the fertility tradition in which the Druid or Lord of the Dance played a vital part, and which reaped the immediate and vehement condemnation of all churches dedicated to monogamy. Clearly this was the one pagan practice which could not be fully sublimated into a folk tradition, but some parts of it lingered on in dancing round the Maypole and other more innocuous local customs. Thus did our Celtic ancestors worship, and it is against this backcloth of orgies and magic that we must set the perilous achievement of men like Patrick, Berach and Molaise.

Off the south coast of Boa lies an archipelago of nine islands. The nearest, Lustybeg, was the home of the recluse, Ned Allingham, who was a brother of the poet, and chose to live and die on this island rather than follow William to the honours and worries of fame in London. The largest of the group is Lustymore which once belonged to the Acheson family, who built a magnificent house on it with a view across the lake to the Poola Fooka range which could have few rivals in Britain. The Achesons departed some fifty years ago and the roof has fallen in, leaving only the gaunt walls crowned by pointed supports for gables. The remains of a fine lawn stretched out in front of a small summerhouse, but the rest of the island was lost in a tangle of briars and undergrowth.

To the north-west, between Sallow and Lustybeg islands lies a small rock called Purgatory where the Stations of the Cross were performed, and for many years it was a rival to the purgatory on Little Lough Derg, to the north; on the same island was a large slab of rock known as the Altar, which may have been a pagan burial stone. The navigation around the Lusty archipelago is rocky and complicated, and should not be attempted without accurate charts. Though we could not find it, we were told that one of the islands in this archipelago contained rocks which had once been molten from some volcanic upheaval, and their surface bears the imprint of the feet of large prehistoric mammals.

There is reasonably deep water under the bridges at both ends of Boa Island and the border of the Republic runs down to the lake for a few hundred yards on the north shore. This boundary has a diocesan origin, enabling pilgrims who travelled along the Way of the Saints to be protected as they landed at the port by the MacGraths, who were the Wardens of the Lough Derg sanctuary and had a castle nearby. This was no doubt a lucrative hereditary post, and was last held by Myler MacGrath, a noted "Vicar of Bray" in Elizabethan times, who managed to change his faith to suit his politics on several occasions. The Way of the Saints was therefore a kind of *via franca* or specially protected and robber-free route for pilgrims, and there were many places for them to visit along the waterways, and many tombs and relics to be seen. The Lough Derg purgatory is the last surviving place approved by the hierarchy, but there must once have been a thriving hire-boat trade to cope with so many visitors, for the Irish are among the world's most inveterate pilgrims.

Chapter 14

CIRCUMNAVIGATING ENNISKILLEN

WE sailed from Goblusk Bay one misty morning when the lake was perfectly still and even the birds had not woken, leaving a broadening wedge of white water astern. Weaving our way among the islands past the old site of Castle Hume we glimpsed the conical cap of the eleventh-century round tower of Devenish standing 81 feet high and almost piercing the clouds beyond the bare brow of the hill. This is a perfect specimen which has retained its roof, and it seems to carry the eye towards the heavens much as the spires of some churches and the perpendicular architecture of others draw the mind up and away from earthly things. As we watched the clouds sailing behind the tower it gave the illusion of moving like a giant stylus, writing its way across a white parchment of cloud and registering still, after more than a thousand years, the act of faith which had once assembled, polished and joined together those vast quantities of stone to create the spiritual lighthouse of this remote and barely accessible island.

The founder of Devenish was St. Molaise, one of the Twelve Apostles of Ireland, who died about 563; he was descended from the ruling house of Ulster on his father's side, and through his mother from the Kings of Tara. There is a tenuous link between Molaise and the *torc-tened* or sacred sun-flame, for when he visited Tara one winter for an Assembly his hut was the only one on which the snow melted, since the warmth of his grace extended, it was said, even to the building above him – a possible transference to a Christian leader of the hero-light associated with warriors like Cuchulain. Heroism was considered, probably rightly, to be largely the product of heredity and of environment, and was associated with light and the sun, so we find Molaise described by St. Cormac as "a king's son of reddened valour".

Indirectly Molaise was responsible, the legends claim, for the foundation of the famous monastery of Iona, off Mull, in Scotland, for about 560 Columba gained access to a book belonging to St. Finian of Moville and sought to transcribe it. Manuscripts were extremely precious and closely guarded in the days before printing – indeed, some of them were the labour of a lifetime – and Finian refused permission. The appeal to King Diarmait resulted in his famous judgement "To every cow belongs her calf and to every book its son-book". Columba, raging with unpriestly fury at this, went off to raise his father's clan, and defeated King Diarmait at the Battle of Cooldrevny, near Lough Gill in 560, and the slaughter on both sides was considerable. Columba, his anger cooling to shame, sought spiritual guidance from St. Molaise who laid on his penitent the sad but necessary banishment with the added condition that he should seek to convert as many souls to the faith as had been slaughtered in the war. From this little seed of penitence, sown on the peaceful isle of Devenish grew the great monastery of Iona which converted many of the Irish conquerors of the Picts, and also a young prince called Oswald who was to bring St. Aidan south to show the pagan Saxons of Northumbria in the seventh century the way to a richer religion and a more honourable ethic.

St. Maedoc of Ferns was Molaise's friend and frequent companion on the Way of the Saints. The old chronicles tell us that these two companions were sheltering one day during their travels beneath two branching trees near Tullyhaw in County Cavan, and began to discuss how they should follow their vocations. Gradually the roots of these trees began to creak and groan until they fell apart, one tumbling to the north, and the other pointing south. "By the fall of these trees," said Maedoc, "it has been revealed that we must part," and so he went south to found his abbey at Ferns in Leinster while Molaise went north to found Devenish. The tale has of course its inner kernel of hard fact, that in the conversion of a partly pagan nation the exigencies of the service demanded personal hardships and sacrifices.

Yet Maedoc often visited Molaise at Devenish. In one tale we find him travelling late and footsore over the mountainous Slieve

Beagh on the borders of Fermanagh and Monaghan and utterly lost in a difficult country full of wild beasts, but soon, the tale tells us, two angels picked him up in their hands and deposited him safe and sound at his destination in the royal fortress. On another occasion three children were drowned in Lough Erne and their bodies could not be found, but their mother went around the local saints pathetically begging them to help her. A separate guest-house with a private garden was maintained at Devenish for Maedoc so that he could visit the island with his followers as often as he wished, stay as long as he liked, and be certain of comfortable quarters however crowded the place might be.

So when Maedoc arrived on his next visit the woman came to him weeping and said, "My son has been drowned in the lake, and two other children with him, and I and his father Eochaid, chief of this land, are going to all the saints hoping to learn where we can find his body." The two set out and searched the waters carefully but could find no trace of the missing children, so at length St. Maedoc went down to the shore and prayed, stretching out his hand, "O Jesus," he said, "raise up for me the son of this woman and the other bodies with him." The surface of the water rippled and gradually the three drowned children rose out of it, dazed but alive and well.

A tale of one of Maedoc's most charming miracles relates how he had climbed away to a remote wood near Lough Erne to read the psalms when a hunted stag with the hue and cry close behind it floundered into the clearing and stood exhausted by his side. Maedoc gently placed his rosary over the antlers and when the hounds drew up they could neither see nor scent the deer, but thought that there were two men standing there, so they sniffed the air and whined a little until they were called off. Before it trotted away the stag laid the rosary reverently at the feet of the saint.

On another occasion, while Maedoc was visiting Saint David in Wales, a man who hated him for his holiness sent him off on an absurd errand with another surly fellow who was instructed to murder him. St. Maedoc went willingly, leaving the book that he was studying in the open, and when they reached a

Devenish Island on lower Lough Erne

remote place the assassin raised his axe, but suddenly his hands stuck fast to the haft and he was unable to move a muscle, so there they stayed, the saint rapt in contemplation and the murderer frozen in the act until St. David and his brethren eventually discovered them, but when Maedoc returned to his book, although it had rained heavily, not a drop had touched the parchment.

There are few more delightful comradeships than that of the 'Four Musketeers' of the early Celtic Church, Maedoc, Molaise, Caillin and Ultan, and when eventually they journeyed together to Rome, all the bells of that city, it was said, rang out in a great carillon of their own accord, to honour the devoutest band of pilgrims that had ever come from Ireland.

Devenish is a good place to ask oneself what it was like to live in these monastic isles during that golden age from about 500 to 850 when the scholars and craftsmen and theologians raised the Irish nation to the zenith of its achievement. Certainly the founding of a monastery called for a disciplined and capable administrator. This founder saint would begin by praying and fasting for forty days and nights, and blessing the place to dispel its Druidical associations, and then the enclosure of the land granted by the local king or chieftain would be walled in like a fort, possibly with three concentric walls, but often with only one. Then the cemeteries were laid out – an important item because places had to be chosen on these rocky islets where there was sufficient depth of earth for decent burial. Then the saint built his own oratory, and if he had followers, marked out places for his brethren to construct their churches and wooden cells covered with wattles and thatch. Later came the round towers, built partly as belfries, lookout posts and sanctuaries against hostile raiders, and partly perhaps because the more contemplative orders enjoyed the wonderful views from the top. The conical roofs of these towers presented considerable problems and called for extremely precise measurement. Most of the round towers were constructed as later additions between the eighth and the eleventh century.

Then the founder would ordain and set in order the priests and lay brethren, and issue rules for the students, each man being directed to work which suited his character and skills. Hospitality was important, and also the care of the sick and needy in the parish and surrounding countryside. The early monasteries were almost always placed on the sites of Druid sanctuaries and 'universities'; this was clearly a policy of the early Celtic Church in its determination to replace paganism with a more rewarding ethic.

On one side was a thatched house of wood, the monastic school, where students scribbled on small pieces of slate or stone, or on wax tablets, for parchment was too precious for practice, using an iron stylus. It would call for years of patient study before a few specialists could graduate to illuminating the gospels, psalms or early historical documents. Learning was pursued for its own sake, there were no prizes, degrees or scholarships, and Bede tells us that English pupils were taken in, educated, fed and supplied with books entirely free of charge. There was generally a senior lecturer and professors of law, Greek, Latin, poetry, history and other disciplines, while a steward managed the organization of the community. Others studied the craft of carving, generally learning on animal bones to create the incredibly delicate interwoven designs of Celtic gold, silver and bronze-ware, a craft which had flourished in Ireland since neolithic times. If they did so well with metal, their wood carving must have been superb, but it has scarcely survived. Most priests carried bells which were made at the monasteries, and were riveted, though by the tenth century technical advances enabled them to be cast. It was in these little monastic foundries that the miracles of Celtic metal-work were created – croziers, shrines for books and relics, intricately-worked crosses like that of Cong, powerful interwoven clasps for the books, and brooches to gather up cloaks and kilts. By the tenth century they were making bronze needles which closely resemble the modern steel product. The Celtic monastery was therefore a very practical institution. It played an important part in local politics and a vital part in civilizing the country; it was a powerful blend of the scientific and the spiritual, of the theological college and the technical institution.

Sundials kept the time, and in winter when there was less sun the problem was overcome by shortening each hour until some of them might last only forty minutes, but in summer it could stretch to eighty minutes. A similar time system is still used by some monasteries and fits in with the communal prayers every three hours – Prime or Mattins at sunrise, Terce at the third hour, Sext at the sixth; at the ninth hour, None, and the twelfth, Duodecima or vespers.

Though life for the lay brethren was not too grim the monks formed a *corps d'élite* which was supposed to, and often did, live up to startlingly high standards of asceticism. Spells were particularly frowned on and if any cleric or woman used magic to lead a person astray they had to spend three years on a diet of bread and water and a further three years abstaining from meat and wine. Corporal punishment was used, at least in the earlier communal rules, so that smiling or coughing during prayers was punishable with six blows. Such a high standard of mortification was often achieved that it was not surprising that many of the earlier monks were called saints. Some of these practices of abnegation were inherited, like the Celtic tonsure, from the Druids, for the Church found that it could not be outdone by the rival firm; one penance consisted of lying in cold water on a bed of nettles for a night or so, which must surely have been inducive to coughing in Chapel the next day, and many of the saints stood up to their waists in icy water for hours on end to mortify the flesh. Another penance was a night of vigil in the mortuary with a corpse as companion. Inevitably such high standards could not be sustained indefinitely by many, and after 200 years or so, much-needed reforms were being introduced.

Such highly educated, dedicated and single-minded men were inevitably powerful and greatly influenced the rulers of the land, but as time passed the abbots were too regularly appointed because of their kinship with the local kings or chieftains. The monastic finances were gathered largely from the offerings of pilgrims, and as time wore on some delightful but very dubious tales of the patron saints were written merely as publicity gimmicks to attract larger numbers of paying visitors. A tithe was collected from the local people by travelling around the parishes bearing the relics of the saints, who demanded their dues much as the King of Tara demanded his when he travelled on his itineraries.

In St. Michael's Roman Catholic Church at Enniskillen you can see a statue of St. Molaise carrying in his left hand the Devenish Gospel Shrine, one of the beautiful early book cases which have been found in recent years. Another, the Cumdach, an eleventh-century copy of an earlier book shrine is a small bronze box plated with silver and ornamented with gilt patterns, and was made by Cennfailad who was Abbot of Devenish from 1001 to 1025. The moulding of the gilt was his workmanship also and the box is preserved in the National Museum, Dublin.

The main difference between Continental and Celtic monasticism was that the houses under Roman sway existed within the organization of the Church, but Irish monasticism virtually *was* the Church. The many small oratories on these early sites evolved because the men who built them did not possess the architectural skill to construct a single large building of stone, though they certainly could have created a very large hall of timber; in the place of one central abbey they therefore built six or seven small oratories without windows in which the altar candles generally provided the only light. The larger churches on Devenish, Inchcleraun and Inchagoill were added later as building techniques improved.

While the Celtic Church in England ceased to exist as a separate entity soon after the Council of Whitby in 664, in Ireland it has been generally accepted that it did not long survive the Synod of Kells in 1152, but Mary Rogers has produced fascinating evidence to show that it survived in a tenuous form on the isle of Devenish until the monks were ejected in 1603. The order of the Culdees or Companions of God was founded by Mael-Ruain as a reform movement towards the close of the eighth century and spread to Glasgow and to Caernarvonshire. It was a stern order, mostly vegetarian, which sought to revive the high standards of Celtic asceticism, a hundred blows on the hand being only part of the penance for a priest who was angry with a servant. Devenish became a Culdee monastery soon after the order started, and though an Augustinian order based on the Roman system was later introduced into the island, the Culdees continued and co-habited with them until the local dissolution of monasteries in 1603. They were therefore a separate order under their own prior, and Killadeas on the eastern shore of the lake is named after them.

The approach to Enniskillen by water is superb. Beyond Devenish the navigation narrows between two close-set marker posts, hard by a shoal of four rocks in a line called Friar's Leap. The tale told of these perilous rocks is, one suspects, of quite recent origin, but refers to the early monastic days. A young friar was sitting on the mainland reading the Psalms when he suddenly glanced up to see the Lady of the Lake, the entrancing blonde mermaid who is reputed to inhabit the deep places of Lough Erne, seated on the farthest rock and beckoning to him. Overcome by a purely scientific curiosity he waded out to the end of the shoal but when he clambered up the mermaid vanished and her place was taken by the Devil himself, horns, hoofs, tail and all, and a powerful stench of sulphur thrown in for good measure. The friar was so frightened that he leapt from rock to rock with the Devil literally hot on his trail, and he never stopped until he was over the old causeway which once linked Devenish to the mainland on the eastern shore. If you doubt the veracity of this tale you may inspect the groove in the rock where the Devil's hooves skidded, and so it was that this shoal acquired the name of the Friar's Leap.

The deep gorge just below The Royal School at Portora was a natural ford for many centuries before the bridges were built and the scene of many battles. When the navigation channel was deepened stone and bronze weapons were found embedded in the silt, and some of them can be seen in the Belfast Museum. On the right bank rise the ruins of the typical plantation tower-house of Portora which was built by Sir William Cole before 1618, and was briefly a Bishop's Palace. The only lock on the navigation helps to control the supply of water for the power stations below Belleek, and since the levels were almost identical the keeper waved us through without any need to operate it.

Beyond the gorge we saw the towers and spires of Enniskillen standing out against the sky. Viewed from downstream it is probably the most picturesque town on any waterway in Britain for most of it is still contained on Kathleen's Island from which it takes its name; Kathleen, a lady strictly in the Maeve tradition, was said to have slain a King of Formorians at the Second Battle of Moytura, near Lough Corrib. The old port of the town, last used for trading when John MacManus ran a cargo of sand up from Lustybeg Island about 1928, lies near the southern tip of the island.

The Water Gate at Enniskillen, built about 1580, is a fine example of part of one of the few mortared stone castles constructed by clan chieftains in Ireland and is best seen from the river. A junior branch of the Maguire clan kept an almost royal state there, for Celtic society was essentially aristocratic in organization. They ruled the waters of the lake with a private navy of about 1,500 boats, partly stationed at Enniskillen, where the poet O'Higgins described the "Grove of tapering shipmasts", and partly at Bannagh Bay, near Hare Island. In 1369 the Maguires put this fleet to the test when they defeated the O'Donnells in a naval battle on the Broad Reach, and with their victory avenged the killing of Muldoon, who was an ally of their sept.

It is interesting to compare the City of God on Devenish with the City of this world at the Maguire fortress where the smiths and braziers fashioned the spears and swords and blazoned shields, the Scottish masons hammered away at the stones for the castle and the beautiful women of the court wove golden tapestries depicting, perhaps, the thrilling hunt of the wild boar. Poets recited and minstrels sang and the fighting men feasted and rode out to raid their neighbours' cattle and settle ancient blood feuds. On Devenish peace and prayer and order reigned, and beautiful things were created, but in the Maguire rath lay the pomp and circumstance of this more transitory world, which was sadly rewarded in 1439 when the chief was captured in his own castle.

About 1590 the fortress was stormed by the Elizabethan settlers, and was later retaken by the Maguires, though by 1607 it was firmly in the hands of Sir William Cole, the founder of modern Enniskillen, who rebuilt it. One of the first tasks of the settlers was to achieve naval supremacy on the lakes and it seems likely that shallow-draught men-of-war were armed with small culverins, for a document of 1611, referring to the castle, states that "The King has three good boats there ready to attend all services".

Moving upstream from the water gate we turned to port and passed along the western and southern side of the town until our way was barred by a broad road bridge with closely-set concrete slabs running into the water. As the current pushed us down on to these piers it seemed that there was no space for our boat to slip through and with a mighty crunch we struck the sharp edge of the support a glancing blow which deposited the skipper and first mate in a tangled pile by the cabin door.

By this time the *Mary Ann* was slewed across the piers with the current piling up on the starboard side and some rather un-theological remarks rising to the ears of the citizens of Enniskillen, who were peering over the side and wondering what we were doing to their bridge. Several frantic shoves with the boat hook and a line on the concrete carried the stern around, and we rocked through the widest gap with rather less than a quarter of an inch to spare on either side, and considerably more water in the bilge than we had started with. As we curved back to the port to complete our circumnavigation of the town we surveyed the damage and found that our main loss was paint scraped from the starboard bow, but I would not care to make the voyage again in anything larger than a canoe.

Above Enniskillen we moved through a countryside of broad and placid water meadows until we arrived at the piers of the abandoned railway viaduct of the old Sligo, Leitrim and Northern Counties line. On the left bank lay a fine stone quay where we moored and walked up the drive to Castle Coole. As we came over the brow of the hill we saw outlined against the clouds and trees one of the finest houses in the classical style that you could find anywhere in the British Isles. There are plenty of others which are larger and more impressive, but the proportions of Castle Coole are superb. It was built by James Wyatt and is a late example of his classical work, for he turned to Gothic when he rebuilt Ashridge in Hertfordshire for George,

173

Lord Gower, the future Duke of Sutherland. Indeed, Wyatt's classical work seems to have been of a different standard to his Gothic, for his restorations of some of our churches and cathedrals earned him the unhappy title of "the destroyer"! The stone for Castle Coole was carried by ship all the way from Portland to Ballyshannon, overlanded past the rapids, and transported by barge to the fine quay at which we had moored, where it was transferred to carts to bring it to the site, which had once been the rath of the hereditary physicians of the Maguire chiefs. The house was built for the first Earl of Belmore from 1790–98, and was later handed over to the National Trust.

Chapter 15

THE HAUNTED LAKE

CLOSE to Castle Coole and a little way upstream on the right there is a private house which peers out rather shyly from a shelter of trees and contains some remnants of one of the greater abbeys on the Erne Navigation. Lisgoole was founded by the Maguires in 1106 and was the burial place of the senior branch of that clan. It began as an Augustinian house but was handed over to the Franciscans about 1581. The Annals of the Four Masters mentions an unfortunate accident in 1516 when a cot in which two members of this community, Walter Walsh and Teige O'Higgins were sailing, overturned and drowned them both. Michael O'Cleery, chief of the scribes known as the Four Masters, came to Lisgoole after the Dissolution of the Monasteries, found shelter nearby with some of his dispersed Franciscan brethren and wrote the Book of the Invasions. Though this is an extremely mythological early history of Ireland gathered from a variety of not very reliable sources it still contains much material of value to historians. Lisgoole was originally planned as the county town of Fermanagh, but the site was changed to Enniskillen because the castle on the island was a more practical place to defend.

We must at times have presented a curious spectacle as we threaded our way by boat across the Irish countryside. The cramped quarters at the stern meant that after an hour or two our legs were so hot from their proximity to the engine that we had to take off our shoes and socks and dangle our feet in the water to get them cool again. If it was also rainy weather, as it often was, we would unfurl the umbrella over our heads, and the finished spectacle, though practical enough under the circumstances was hardly one which would have met with the approval of the stewards at Henley.

There are thirteen miles of water between Enniskillen and the upper lake and beyond Lisgoole we entered a weird countryside

175

in which the river wound among a maze of headlands and islands studded with hummocks which closely resembled gigantic plum-puddings turned upside-down – the drumlins left behind by the slow erosion of glaciers – some of them standing several hundred feet high. There is such a maze of channels and small lakes in this area that we had been advised to keep to the right all the way up to Knock Island and then pass either side of Inishmore, since both channels are navigable. Though it is hard to distinguish Cleenish Island from the river, it was once a famous monastic school when the ascetic Sinall, son of Manacus lived there in the sixth century. He was known as the wisest man in Ireland, which was no small distinction at that time, and was the tutor of St. Columbanus who was one of the greatest missionaries of the Celtic Church. Columbanus was born in 543 and studied at Cleenish before graduating to St. Comgall's theological college at Bangor. Columbanus formed the spearhead of the Irish mission to Europe during the Dark Ages, when he founded Annegray and Luxeuil monasteries in France, and Bobbio in the Appenines. A Gaelic rowing song sometimes attributed to this saint records a storm encountered in a small boat on the Rhine:

> *The winds raise blasts, wild rain-storms wreak their spite*
> *But steady strength of men subdues it all —*
> *Heave men and let resounding echo sound our heave.*

One cannot help hearing behind such a refrain faint echoes of the later Eton Boating Song.

Mr. and Mrs. Hubert Brown welcomed us most hospitably when we reached Carry Bridge; their house stands near to its broad span, and we felt that we were again getting close to the border when they told us that it was not so many years since the I.R.A. had blown it up, leaving them with a considerable bill to pay for repairs to their windows.

This bridge is really the beginning of the upper lake, and on a warm and sunny morning we set off to explore what promised to be a very different waterway, with few open stretches and a multitude of closely-packed islands. About fifteen of these are still inhabited though we were told that some were only used during a part of the year. Then a sudden bend in the river revealed the startling outline of Knockninny Hill which is not very tall, but the sides are bare and barren rock blasted by wind and rain and cracked by frost until it resembles an outcrop of the Sahara, carved into uncanny shapes by the processes of erosion. A film of mist hung round the summit, lending it a majestic air of shrouded mystery. Beyond lay the taller range of the Slieve Rushen, riding 1,300 feet along the horizon but by comparison a mere backcloth, far less impressive than Knockninny.

Belle Isle emerged on our left, a large island with several farms on it, and across a long lagoon we saw the old house built close to the site of the monastery in which Cathal Macmanus wrote most of the *Book of Senad of MacManus of Lough Erne*, commonly known as *The Annals of Ulster*, during the fifteenth century; this is a vital and reasonably accurate history recording important events in the North from 431 to 1131 and from 1155 to 1541, and the key manuscript is preserved in the library of Trinity College, Dublin. MacManus, who was born in 1439 was able to combine the duties of vicar of Inishkeen and Dean of the rural deanery of Lough Erne with the hereditary chieftainship of his branch of the clan Maguire. He was a married Roman Catholic priest at a time when the tradition of married clergy lingered on from the more lenient customs of the Celtic Church. His son Thomas, who succeeded him as chieftain described him as "one who was full of grace and knowledge in every science, both law and theology, physic and philosophy, and knowledge of Gaelic also".

The old name of Belle Island was Shanid, which suggests that synods of the Church were held there and there was probably a small castle on this site even before the days of the Plantation. It was from this house that John Vesey Porter ran his own fleet of steamships, which was sometimes known rather blasphemously, as the Royal Erne Navy. He also played an important part in adjusting the water levels of the lakes; before this in the 1880's it was often said that Lough Erne was in Fermanagh during the summer, and that Fermanagh was in Lough Erne during the winter. Two families, the Irvines and the Porters were foremost in this work of opening flooded land to the benefits of agriculture, and their achievement is marked by two plaques, one between Belle Isle and the mainland, and the other on the shore below the Irvines' old home at Rockfield, on the lower lake.

Porter not only ran his own newspaper, but supplied a fascinating route to Dublin which can have had few rivals for complexity. At Enniskillen the passengers could purchase a through ticket to Dublin on board the steamship *Knockninny* which departed at 7.00 a.m. for Belturbet. There they disembarked into carriages which took them by road to Cavan in time to catch the afternoon train to Dublin. The traveller must have arrived a little weary in the old capital but there can be few transport tickets of that date which included three separate methods of propulsion.

As we rounded the western point of Belle Isle an extraordinary jumble of islands opened out before us. The upper lake is best compared with a vast jigsaw-puzzle which a child has scattered petulantly, but close together. The islands tend to look as though they ought to fit tightly and drive the Erne out through a subterranean channel, and there are only a few wide open stretches of water – compared with most of the lakes that we had explored it was a safe navigation, but we learned later of some notable storms on some of the broader reaches.

With all our hard-won knowledge of Irish waterways we believed that we could scarcely get lost on one, so we turned between Inishleague and Mountjoy Island with the intention of running down the centre of the lake, but soon we were completely bewildered. On the map the islands were clearly of different shapes and sizes, but seen from the boat they all looked much the same and it became impossible to tell where headlands ended and the lake began. Gradually the channel ahead grew narrower until we realized that we had reached the western shore; we learned later that we had passed between Inishlught and the mainland and were fortunate that the water level was high since there is seldom depth enough there for anything larger than a dinghy. A little way inland was a cottage where the pigs were so surprised at seeing us that they rushed down knee-deep into the water to inspect us more closely.

178

Passing north of Inishcreevan we saw Inishturk rising almost 200 feet from the water ahead with a small white cottage close to the summit; as it was near the centre of the lake we began to regain our sense of direction and found deep water close in on the north-western shore. There we moored and sat down to lunch in the sunshine on the benches of an old hulk. As we were eating we heard someone whistling as he walked down the hill, and suddenly over the top of the gate appeared a postman in full uniform with his mailbag flung over his shoulder. William Rooney told us that he delivered mail to the islanders by boat three days a week and spent the other three days taking it around the farms and houses on the mainland. In the winter he said that there were times when he found it difficult to get his boat through the ice, but he seldom failed to ensure that letters and parcels reached their destinations on time. His father William had also delivered the mail for forty-five years using a sailing boat, but he himself had a small outboard when not rowing. His pillar-box red skiff, a little faded in colour by the Atlantic gales, was moored by the shore and we caught a colour photograph of it as he rowed away on his eight-mile rounds to the south.

There was a tragic sequel to this brief encounter. Two years later we were staying at the Rock Hotel in Gibraltar over Christmas, and often sitting out on the balcony of our room in the sun while Britain was gripped in one of the iciest winters for a number of years. I glanced quickly through a newspaper and my eye was suddenly caught by a headline which I read all too quickly. It described how William Rooney was on his way home to his wife and two children on Inishturk after completing his Christmas rounds when his boat was locked into the ice. As he became clearly overdue his brother James, realizing the risk of death from exposure, set out to rescue him, but the iron grip of the ice tightened around his boat also. The two brothers were found later frozen to death only a short distance apart from each other. The post continues to be delivered by boat on Upper Lough Erne, and John, another member of the Rooney family is responsible for it, but the little mail-boat is now equipped with distress rockets and a lifebelt.

We emerged from the complications of the upper lake at Lady Craigavon Bridge after passing to the north of Trannish Island, and on the east shore found a fine, gently sloping stone jetty reaching down into the water, and some two hundred yards off it the small circular island of Inisrath, well planted with trees.

The large and well-maintained private house on Inisrath was built by one of the Cavendish Butler family about 1844 and in those days before the Celtic revival the place was known to the locals more prosaically as Rabbit Island. There was a rath, or old fort, near the centre, which was the obvious site to build on but it was covered with a dense matting of thorn trees which were then, and indeed often still are, sacrosanct to the Irish, and none of the men working on the site would touch them, so Mr. Butler had to set to and grub them out himself before foundations could be laid. By that time it was winter and there followed one of those desperately hard frosts which proved so fatal to the Rooney family; the Erne froze almost solid but this proved a blessing for all the building materials were carried across the ice, which must have been deep indeed to support horses and carts filled with such heavy goods.

Beyond Inisrath the Erne opens once more into one of the loveliest, wildest and most strangely haunted waterways in the world. While Lough Ree has its monster and its banshee and the lower lake its mermaid, Upper Lough Erne boasts two even stranger apparitions. In this age when we read so much about unidentified flying objects it is intriguing to encounter such a fully documented unidentified skimming object as the weird 'light' of the upper lake. A completely trustworthy first-hand description of this phenomenon was sent me by Major Henry Cavendish Butler who was brought up on Inisrath. In 1913 he was bicycling back from Lisnaskea at night with the late George Beresford and, in his own words :

The night was glassy calm and when we got to Derryadd Quay we could see the whole of the Gehan (the northern tip of Dernish Island) lit up as if it were floodlit from behind – you could see every branch. We watched it all the time as we rowed across to Inisrath, but the trees prevented us seeing the point of light so we cycled as fast as possible up the drive 'till we could look up the lake – it took us only two or three minutes, but when we got to the far side of the island, all was black. We went up to the house and told my wife we had seen the light, and I went over and pulled up the blind. For a second or two Riley Point, about one mile up the lake, lit up and then went out. What shook me was the brightness – a diffused glare like the largest of car headlamps. The head gardener at Crom, who also saw it, described it as an enormous orange ball which came from under the bridge to the Garden Island, and lit up all the yachts which were then anchored in Crom Bay. In those days I had the fastest motorboat on Lough Erne and I said to Pat Goodwin I should like to chase the light, but he replied, "If it was really going, sir, you'd never catch it!"

Another visitation had occurred in 1912. While looking out of a window of Crom Castle, Florence, Lady Erne saw a very bright light moving quickly up the river towards the farm, but apparently making no sound. A party of people being ferried to the Garden Island at Crom on a particularly wild winter night saw two of these lights rising and falling and travelling both with and against the wind which was blowing the better part of a gale. When Lady Erne asked Pat Goodwin, the head boatman whether he knew of a very fast and silent motor boat with a searchlight he replied that although many people had seen these strange skimming objects, no one had ever discovered their source.

I shall deal rather quickly with the antiquities of the upper lake, partly because the islands are often inhabited and would not therefore welcome too many visitors, and partly because there remains a good deal of research to be done on them. William Rooney lived on Inishturk, which means Boar's Island, and this was probably the local cult site of Manannan Mac Lir, the erstwhile lord and god of these wandering waters. The largest of the Naan Islands has the remains of a plantation castle and Inishroosk a monastery of which St. Berchan was the abbot in the sixth century. Two fine bronze swords found in the lake near Inishleague particularly fascinated me because of their leaf-shaped blades which broaden out from the hilt down and do not begin to narrow until a point quite close to the tip. This is a very ancient and not very practical weapon design for it makes the sword heavy and difficult to fence with, but as a magistrate in Africa I had presided over cases in which blades of an identical kind had been the key exhibits. Manannan Mac Lir's magical sword which slew at a single blow was probably of a very similar design.

Sailing to the east of Inisrath we took the deeper channel west of Dernish and Bleanish islands and came to the glory of the waters around Crom Castle. There are few places where the hand of man has combined with nature to produce such a magnificent effect. Five wooded headlands stretch out into a deep bay. On one point stands the older ruined castle which was surrounded by water until the level of the lake was lowered, a church crowns another cape, and on another is a small and attractive schoolhouse. In one of the southern bays stands a tower built as a Gothick folly, but now sufficiently well weathered to be attractive. In the Castle Bay a fleet of Snipes bobbed at their moorings.

Crom was built by Michael Balfour in 1611 as a plantation castle to command the vital waterway between the two important garrison towns of Belturbet and Enniskillen. About 1655 it passed to Colonel Abraham Crichton who was an ancestor of the present proprietor, Lord Erne. In 1689 during James II's brief struggle in Ulster it resisted a siege by Lord Galmoy at the head of an undisciplined and poorly armed band of Jacobite recruits. It was staunchly defended and though the garrison lacked cannon they were highly skilled marksmen with the long duck guns which they mounted on double rests on the battlements. It was with one of these that they managed to wound Galmoy himself while he was carrying out a reconnaissance about a mile away. Soon after this the siege was raised and though it was renewed later on the defenders held out until relief came from Enniskillen.

During the siege two men crept out at night and buried all

the family treasure and plate in the grounds. Though it was known where these valuables were hidden it was not divulged, for it was said that whenever anyone went to dig it up, blood always flowed. In 1930 there was a strange sequel to this tale when an old estate carpenter summoned several of the Crichton family to meet him. Just as he was about to tell them where the treasure lay their favourite greyhound crawled up with blood pouring from a very deep gash and had to be hurried away at once to the vet.

According to an ancient book "It is usual for gentlemen sailing by this place to discharge some guns in compliment to the venerable castle," a tribute perhaps to the erstwhile marksmanship of its defenders. Though the *Mary Ann* carried no armaments we paid the ancient ruin a strident salute on our fog-horn which we hoped would serve in lieu of musketry. The whole area around Crom is well-wooded with oak and ash, yew and larch and pine carefully planted and huddling down to the water's edge from the multitude of islands and headlands of all shapes and sizes, but as in most forests there is one tree which is monarch of all around it and this Irish yew grows in the courtyard of Crom Castle. Even in 1794 the branches spread so wide that it was claimed that it would be capable of sheltering all the members of the Parliament at Westminster. Much as the tree must have grown since then with aging branches tenderly supported on upright poles, the supreme legislature has evolved even faster, and one doubts if it could still accommodate all our M.P.'s.

Crom also has its private leprechaun which has been seen often and by many people. One September evening about 1907, just as it was getting towards dusk a French maid and Lord Erne's very matter-of-fact governess were rowing from Lanesborough Lodge, when they saw the small figure of a man walking on the water from the direction of the castle past the ferry towards Corlat. The governess saw him first but said nothing, being afraid to tell the maid for fear that she might panic, but shortly afterwards the Frenchwoman also saw it clearly. When they landed, Lord Erne questioned each of them separately and their descriptions tallied in every respect. When the new castle was built the site had to be altered because it was regarded as 'unlucky', and the workmen's tools were disturbed whenever they left them, by unseen forces. Miss Ringwood, the daughter of a former chaplain at Corlat claimed to have seen the leprechaun frequently. It would, she said, walk into her bedroom which was on the ground floor, and sit on the chest-of-drawers and smile at her!

About 1790 the Earl of Erne was returning by ship from a house-warming party at Florencecourt. As his barge was being rowed through the upper lake they saw a strange orange glow on the far horizon, like an enormous fire. This was not one of the weird lights of Upper Lough Erne, for as they rounded the bay their worst fears were confirmed: the old castle at Crom was wrapped in sheets of flame. Like so many houses in Ireland it had been burnt down by accident, but a new house was built nearby; this in its turn was burned to the ground by accident, and an urgent message was sent to Lord Erne saying: "Your castle has burned down." To which he is reputed to have returned the even more succinct reply, "Build it up again!" This was done on a handsome scale, but the present castle, in a mild form of Gothic will require the erosion of a few more centuries of wind and frost before it rivals the beauty of what little remains of the old one.

After Crom we were once again lost in a maze of channels and islands where the lack of an adequate chart was a severe handicap. We set off to discover that once-busy industrial terminus where the Ulster Canal locked down into the Erne Navigation at Wattle Bridge. Galloon Island, which lay on our route has two high crosses – these were not generally marks of burial, though nowadays they are often found in cemeteries, but indicate places of particular sanctity – sometimes the site of the original wattle church of a founder saint whose very name has been lost in the mists of antiquity; yet a high cross generally denoted an important and wealthy monastic community.

Galloon, linked to the mainland by a bridge but lost among the mazes of the upper lake, was founded by St. Tierney, a godson of St. Brigit of Kildare, but he moved on later to initiate another house at Clones. Amongst his many miracles Tierney's prayers saved some of the lay brethren from drowning during a severe storm on the lake, and so an appeal to him is still held to be valid in preserving one from drowning on the upper reaches of the Erne.

Father James Clarke who was parish priest of Galloon about 1854 assisted at the marriage of a Protestant girl to a Roman Catholic, was indicted under the harsh Penal laws, and fled abroad to avoid prosecution. At that time the racing of large yachts on the lake was at its zenith and there was a deep rivalry between Crom and Castle Saunderson; the Earl of Erne was determined to win the next vital race at all costs and promised his crew that they could have whatever they asked for if his yacht came first across the line. When the Crom colours were victorious the boatmen reminded the Earl of his promise and asked that he should use his influence to see that Father Clarke returned to his parish. Though the priest did come back and lived on to a ripe old age the tall ships which once sailed the upper lake will never return, for the land drainage work begun about 1880 lowered the levels so much that there are only limited areas where a deep keel could travel safely.

Castle Saunderson, a late Gothic Revival building and formerly one of the great houses on the Erne Navigation lies just across the border beyond Wattle Bridge, but is now a charred and empty ruin.

As we wandered on through those labyrinthine mazes of water we entered a broad lake which seemed by every logic of map-reading to lead away south and east, but as we drew towards the end of it we realized that it could not lead anywhere, for it was blocked with a barrier of stones. Later we learned that this was the Bloody Pass where, in a considerable skirmish the Williamite forces pursued a band of Jacobites into the water with cries of "No Popery, no quarter, no mercy," and killed so many of them before their officers could call them off that the lake around ran red with the blood from their wounds.

The great virtue of the upper lake is that it is so completely wild and isolated – indeed, it is one of the few remaining places in these islands where there is a reasonable degree of privacy, but we had travelled a considerable distance and our fuel supply was running short, so we made our way up a series of back channels until we reached the tall stone quay at Belturbet, which is, by water, some five miles over the border into the Republic. The route we followed was up Foalies' Cut, a straight stretch of canal crossed by a single bridge, which was constructed to link the Ballinamore Canal with Belturbet and so save a long haul round by the Erne River, which is only navigable up to the rapids. Technically, on crossing the border into a foreign country we should have flown the red ensign and a quarantine flag, but even if we had possessed such luxuries the mast of the *Mary Ann* consisted mainly of an old broomstick handle which I had inadvertently sat on while trying to open a tin of baked beans, and was therefore long since out of service. Friends on both sides of the border had in any case warned us that if we were so unwise as to fly any flag at all we would probably be shot at by *both* sides. It was not many years since two local yachts had been riddled with machine-gun bullets below the water-line and had vanished to Manannan Mac Lir's locker.

Belturbet is a thriving little town which is strongly reminiscent of several places in the Italian provinces. Though not quite so large or prosperous as Enniskillen it has clearly benefited considerably from the English fishermen who come over for the pike, perch, bream and rudd which reach record sizes among these meandering lakes and channels. The fall in the levels since the drainage of the land has left the bridge and quay high out of the water, and we found with regret that we drew a little too much to go on upstream and explore Lough Oughter, which must be the least known navigation in these islands. We learned that there was an ample depth of water above the shallows under the bridge, and the Cathedral of Kilmon near Cavan on the eastern shore of this lake should command the respect of all Irish inland navigators, for the first modern canal in the country was constructed near there. Like the Friar's Cut on Lough Corrib it was ecclesiastical in origin. The Bishop of Kilmon, Dr. Timothy Goodwin had his episcopal palace nearby, and appreciated the considerable benefit to local transport and the lake fishermen of a through navigation on Lough Oughter, so at his own expense he had a channel some 500 yards long dug out about 1718, and small trading boats carrying turf and market produce were soon using it.

Castle Hamilton lies on the south-western shore, but the most fascinating fortress in the area is Cloughoughter, a tall circular tower which was once a Reilly stronghold and rises from an island in the centre of the southern end of the lake. It has a stormy history, for in 1369, Philip Maguire took a fleet of cots to besiege the island and liberate the O'Reilly who had been imprisoned there by one of his enemies. During the rising of 1641 the Anglican Bishop Bedell of Kilmore was held on Cloughoughter, and died soon after his release. An excellent pastor who had arranged the translation of the New Testament into Gaelic, he was much respected even by his enemies.

There is an interesting record of an entire monastery of the Premonstratensian order being removed in 1237 from Trinity Island on Lough Key in County Roscommon to one of the islands of Lough Oughter, the grant of land being made by Cathal O'Reilly. As I mentioned earlier, the Franciscans held Trinity Island on Lough Key, so it is likely that that island was unoccupied for a while, since St. Francis died in 1226, and the order did not spread into western Europe immediately.

In 1739 the Rev. Henry wrote of Belturbet that there were "generally some small pleasuring yachts and other boats" riding at anchor there. A boat-hire firm has been established recently, but at the time of our visit this once busy little port had been reduced to a few small fishing skiffs.

From Belturbet we sailed south and west towards the Woodford River. Tall reed rose from the marshy margins and narrow entrances wound away into broad stretches of shimmering lake. All around us the wildfowl, mostly mallard, rose in clouds and the linking lakes must surely be a paradise in winter for anyone with sufficient courage to discharge a gun in an area in which there has been too much shooting of a different kind. We were now running for mile after mile exactly along the border with the Republic on our left and Northern Ireland on our right.

At the first bridge on the Woodford River we moored and walked up the hill to the rounded towers of Auganure Castle, just inside Northern Ireland. The benevolent hand of the Board of Works had not reached its thickset and sturdy battlements, and the courtyard was a mass of briars with saplings sprouting into trees from crevices in the walls. We discovered little of its history but gathered that it was originally a Maguire fortress which was later taken over by the Crichtons.

The sturdy and comfortable old farmhouse of Mr. and Mrs. Bullock near the bridge is an excellent example of a yeoman home, its pleasant garden blending comfortably with the golden honey colour of the deep thatched roof. The bridge in front of it has solid steel stakes driven down through the top so that no vehicle can cross the border, for this is one of the 'unapproved' roads.

We had only to enquire where the Ballinamore Canal began to be invited into the warm and comfortable farm kitchen. For people like these who live alongside the frontier the closing of the side roads is aggravating beyond all measure. Once they could travel a straight four miles to visit friends and relations in the South, but now they have to motor thirty-two miles round by way of an approved road and queue up for customs clearance on the way. The border may be a blessing to the smuggler, but it is a considerable inconvenience to the farmer who has to live beside it.

A relation to our host, Shan, or J. W. Bullock was the chronicler and poet laureate of the upper lake. His father Thomas who lived at Killynick, near Crom, was a Justice of the Peace and land agent to Lord Erne, and Shan emigrated back to England where he spent most of his working life as a civil servant at Somerset House. His main writings on the Erne country are *The Loughsiders*, *The Squireen* and *The Barrys*, and they are filled with vivid portraits of the lives, dialect and customs of those who lived on and around the lake islands. His poetry, *Mors et Vita* was published in 1923, and was written as a tribute on the death of his wife:

> *All that we are and have been*
> *All that we've lived and done,*
> *All that we've said and seen,*
> *Go seeming by and are gone;*

188

THE HAUNTED LAKE

But they live in the ebb and flow
Of life's unfathomed sea —
Life fuller than we know,
Life lovelier than we see.

The Ballinamore and Ballyconnel Canal, to give it the full title, starts at the bridge and we travelled a little way up it to see the first lock, in which the stonework was in good repair though the gates had perished. The river came gushing through the gap in a white flood but some of it was carried away over a stone side-weir into a broad pool shaded by trees. The canal was completed in 1859 and had a very brief official working life to 1869, partly because the dredging was not adequately completed, and partly because the Cavan & Leitrim Light Railway was built along its exact route, with two low bridges which obstructed the navigation. Its affairs were not aided by some of its trustees who seem to have been more interested in steam locomotion than in water transport, and as the exasperated John Porter remarked, "Not in Turkey could there be such a piece of mismanagement as that Ballinamore Canal." Successive writers have revelled in the fact that only eight boats used the navigation during its working life, while the enterprise cost nearly £229,000 to build, but as Mrs. Delany has shown, the truth is that the canal was never made properly navigable because railway interests were already at work planning the route which once ran exactly parallel to the waterway. The Ballinamore is the vital link between the Erne and Shannon Navigations, and it is now not so much a matter of whether it will be reopened, as when, for those who return again for boating holidays will inevitably seek more extensive cruising grounds.

In 1965 the two Tourist Boards in Ireland joined forces to start clearing the canal and it is now navigable up to the lock nearest to the border of the Republic, a distance of some six and a half miles.

The Ballinamore Canal reminds one of the elvers which struggle to get past the concrete walls of the Cathaleen's Fall dam, for long after it was closed yachts regularly attempted to negotiate this uncompleted waterway. One example was an

189

enterprising neighbour of the Butlers at Inisrath, Commander
Gartside-Tipping, who built his own yawl on the upper lake,
and sailed her along the Ballyconnel until he ran aground on the
uncompleted section, where he shipped her out on to a trailer.
Horses drew his large yacht down to the Shannon where he
embarked again. After several weeks exploring the lakes and
islands he locked down into the estuary at Limerick. Beyond
Scattery Island he turned north up the coast and came round to
the mouth of the Erne where he once again embarked on a
trailer for Belleek, continuing his voyage through the lakes until
he reached his home at Rossferry. A man of sterling qualities, he
returned to active service at the age of seventy during the Kaiser's
war, and commanded a minesweeper.

Chapter 16

LAYING UP

THE very vastness of the Erne Navigation offers alternative routes for most voyages, so we returned from Crom by a devious course behind the islands of the eastern shore. Across those hidden and deserted waters sped the gathering arrows of birds preparing for migration while the clouds floated like white wisps of silver splayed on the deep blue dome of the sky. Where Bleanish Island rose 218 feet ahead a skirting of reed ran out from the coastline to greet the green shore, and we moved forward very slowly for fear that we would find no way through, but just as the bow touched the reed we spied a hidden cutting. Autumn was closing in and the dry stalks rustled and chattered high above our heads, rubbing dead leaves together as though they resented our intrusion. As we sailed on cautiously the frightened moorhens scuttled into cover. There was a deep peace as we wound carefully among these tranquil waters, and at the far end an island cottage with a cattle boat drawn up beneath it.

Dernish Island, the next on our course, also has a house on the eastern shore, tucked well away from the prevailing wind. Though these island cottages may lack the amenities of modern life ranging from electricity to piped water and drainage they are mostly owned by those who live in them and remain little kingdoms of independence in a world saturated with conformity.

Returning across the upper lake we passed between Mountjoy Island and Inishleague, leaving Naan and its shooting lodge on our left. Our inclination to return by a different route carried us down a narrow and very shallow inlet between Belle Isle and the mainland, where we found the plaque close to the bridge commemorating John Vesey Porter's work on adjusting the water levels of the navigation. The current soon swept us away from Belle Isle and the haunted upper lake vanished behind us with its extraordinary maze of waters, islands and promontories, but for all its lack of amenities it is still the most remote and un-spoilt navigation that remains accessible.

At Mr. Hubert Brown's jetty we embarked on his fast motor cruiser and returned a little way upstream. Just as the first stars winked out we reached West Island, which is the western continuation of Belle Isle. Mr. and Mrs. John Cathcart live a little way inland from the coast, and he has built boats for many years for the other islanders – mostly the long narrow skiffs which seem best suited to these waters.

We carried away with us from Ireland the golden memory of other evenings as delightful as the one at the Cathcarts with the deep voice intoning more and more improbable tales until one's ribs ached from the sheer surfeit of laughter, for most of us in the east had forgotten the art of the raconteur even before our words were doled out to us by machinery and electricity.

The essence of these Irish tales lies less in the content or context of the story than in the way they are told, so that it is not likely that you will find anything strange in the account of the islander who possessed a higher technical knowledge than his neighbours and set off one night rowing his boat up the lake towards the glimmering light which was shaking down through a fine haze of mist somewhere over beyond Inishore, and himself with only a drop or two inside him, and he rowed as in all his life he had never rowed before until gradually the mist and the water became one and he floated away, and the moon was at first on his right, but later she lay astern of him until at last as he came rowing back as strong as ever, it lay away on his left, and that you see was the first man who ever rowed up and away and around the moon, and returned to tell the tale! There is, as I say, nothing particularly humorous about it all, but we laughed and we went on laughing, for it was told by a man well skilled in the craft of the story-teller. One wishes one could capture a modicum of that secret power of hypnosis which they hold, and transmit it on to paper, as a happier prize than the yellowest crock of gold.

A full moon was riding up the sky as we cruised gently back among the winding banks of Erne with the hunched, uncertain outline of reeds gathering around us, and patches of mist making it difficult to tell exactly where the waters ended and the sky began. The point of that particular tale was driven home, for all along those lakes the mist and the moon combine, reality blends imperceptibly into the intangible, and there is no distinctive boundary between what may, or may not happen next. A small skiff, we felt, could merge all too easily with those banks of cloud until it was floating on waves of mist, beyond the cerulean and still unnavigated vastness of the sky.

Before we left Fermanagh there was, we decided, still one task left undone. The keel of our boat must have passed over many millions of them, but we had never eaten any of the eels which are the main export of the Irish lakes and rivers. The taste for eels increases all the time, but the number available is limited, and gourmets in London and Holland will pay a high price both for the larger ones and for the smaller elvers. At one time they formed a necessary part of the diet of people living on or around the lakes and islands, but we never once saw them included on the menu in any of the hotels at which we stayed.

So when we returned to the lower lake we called on Mr. and Mrs. Johnston on Little Paris, an island which holds no connection with France, being merely an abbreviation for Paradise, which indeed it very closely resembles. The Paradise Islands were used as places of retreat and prayer for pilgrims passing down the Way of the Saints *en route* for Little Lough Derg. On the south side was an anchorage with nets drying in the sun, while half submerged in the water with the warm waves lapping over them lay the broad boxes with holes drilled in the lids in which the eels are kept alive; nearby, an old cattle boat with open planks had been hauled up a little, with the ripples washing over its timbers. Above this rose the green hump of the island with a tidy path and a neat white latched gate leading up to a trim whitewashed cottage with a few small outhouses framed against an orchard heavily loaded with ripe red apples. Here indeed was something closely akin to the Celtic island of Avalon, or apples, where formerly the gods feasted and made merry.

We explained that we were anxious, before we left, to purchase and cook an eel, but Mrs. Johnston would not hear of any such thing. "I don't think," she said, "that you should try cooking an eel unless you've done it before, for it's not so easy as it looks. Come along in now, and I'll fry you one up for your dinner."

It is a complete myth that an eel has to be skinned while alive. As we watched, fascinated, Mrs. Johnston took a sharp knife, cut a slit near the head, and then sliced the neck through, taking care not to cut away any more of the skin. After this she took the two ends of skin near the neck, and with the aid of the knife removed it deftly from the body – this was the most difficult part of the operation which clearly called for some experience. She then carved fillets of the eel from the bone and dropped them into a large frying-pan on the open wood fire, but without including any fat since the eel contains more than enough to prevent it from burning. After about half-an-hour of steady frying she turned them out on to the plates.

Although we were both extremely hungry after a morning spent bobbing in and out among the inlets and islands around Killadeas we were quite unable to finish all that eel between us, and it was not exceptionally large; it tasted extremely good and rather like whiting, though considerably richer.

From Mr. Johnston we learned of how the islanders would sometimes combine for 'round-ups', when they drive the shoals of young perch into corners of the bays until the whole water is a seething mass of small fry hopping on to the shore, and then they sweep them up in very finely meshed nets to use as bait on the long eel lines. We learned also of the small number of eels finding their way up through the new dam at the Cathaleen's Fall and how the stock is gradually decreasing, many of them being old ones now. The fishing policy on the Erne has been to eliminate the pike and so increase the number of trout but once they have gone the perch, which are the pike's natural and main food, increase so considerably that they gobble up much of the young trout spawn. There is therefore a difference of opinion about whether it is wise to dislocate the balance of nature by destroying all the pike. What chiefly impressed me, as one detached from this controversy, was that it could be possible to expunge almost all the pike on such an immense expanse of water as the Erne Navigation. These inland seas breed a variety of unusual species of fish ranging from the pollan, or freshwater herring to mussels, crayfish and shrimps, but the Rainbow trout has only recently been introduced into Fermanagh.

We had now completed our voyage across Ireland from South to North and could go no farther by boat. The time had come to lay up the *Mary Ann*, and with Tom Balfour's help we slipped her on to a small railway truck called, euphemistically, a cradle, and prised her to a snug position against a wall on the site of the old seaplane base. She had carried us in her own peculiarly dangerous fashion over rather more than six hundred miles of mainly turbulent waters, and more than a thousand miles before that when she crossed the British Isles from coast to coast, so that the debt was definitely on our side. We also removed her remarkable engine, the broken down toasting machine, and laid it, a trifle reverently, in the corner of a shed.

To gain a fuller understanding of the Erne Navigation we visited the Cathaleen's Fall dam, named, it is said, after a girl in the Irish resistance who leapt over it to escape from Cromwell's troops, and now the site of a large hydro-electric system. Lower Lough Erne is 152 feet above sea level and its waters are held back, first by the smaller Cliff Power Station just below Belleek, and then by the much larger Cathaleen's Fall dam close to Ballyshannon. Walking into the main hall at the Cathaleen station is like entering into science fiction, for the tall tubular steel turbines have the slightly sinister look of temporarily rested machines from outer space. The dams were completed in 1952 as a joint operation of the two governments, and the Cathaleen unit is so highly mechanized that it is run by only three men. On one side there is a narrow pass with a glass panel in it where we saw the fish working their way up by gradual stages towards their breeding grounds on the upper lakes. Records are kept of the number passing through, the times of day when they come, and the brightness of the sun; few if any fish will pass up the ladder during the hours of darkness, and tall wire nets ring the entrance and the exit to prevent the salmon from committing suicide by leaping out on to dry land, for they will sometimes jump a clear 14 feet, unaware that the Cathaleen's Fall dam looms 148 feet above them. The young elvers cling pathetically around the lower rocks, urged on by an insistent instinct to return to their ancestral breeding grounds but often unable to find any way up the concrete castle. We still know little about the blind force which guides these tiny, almost transparent creatures for anything up to two years on their long migration from the Sargasso Sea across the broad reaches of the Atlantic Ocean. In the deep lock on the Shannon's Ardnacrusha dam as the water is emptied you may see them festooning the sides, clinging in a last spasm of hope to the tiny particles of weed which struggle with a similar optimism for a toehold on life.

Returning by the western shore of the lower lake we paused for a visit to the Marble Arch combe, where the cold mountain river emerges from galleries of caves filled with stalactites, and goes tumbling icy-clear towards the Erne. If one wishes to enter the caves a guide must be taken from Lord Enniskillen's place called Florence Court, which lies a few miles along the road. This small National Trust property is also well worth a visit and is built rather in the style of Gibbs, with colonnades of arches running from the wings to two large summer houses, giving the attractive front an added but unpretentious grandeur. In the grounds stands the ancestor of all the Irish yews, and one of a pair found on the estate about 1770. They are mutations which can only be propagated by cuttings since the seedlings always return to the common type of yew tree.

From there we crossed the border into the wind-blasted, bare and utterly deserted Donegal highlands where the clouds chased each other over the fell as though they were anxious to escape from such a stark and desolate landscape. It was not surprising that it was in the middle of a large mountain tarn in the heart of this savage, though not un-beautiful countryside, that St. Patrick had a vision of Purgatory which has drawn millions of pilgrims down the centuries to this, the last officially approved retreat of the many which once covered the islands of the Ways of the Saints. Immense numbers, mostly Irish, but always including a scattering of foreigners visit it every year, and although Pope Alexander VI decided to close the place in 1497 it continued to be used even through penal times and despite its

196

destruction in 1632. The present pilgrimage lasts about three days, costs £1 and starts at 12.00 p.m. on the evening of departure. The pilgrims arrive at the lake the following morning, are ferried over in rowing-boats and then move around to perform the Stations barefooted. This involves visiting the five round stone circles which mark the beehive huts of the little community which once lived and worshipped on the island; these huts have metal crosses in the centre, and the discipline includes kneeling by them and repeating the Lord's Prayer, Glory be to God and Hail Mary, a set number of times. After two Stations they are provided with a very frugal meal of black tea and toast.

On the second day the pilgrims are allowed to rest in a disciplined fashion, and on the third day they complete two more Stations before returning to the place from which the pilgrimage started. This is not therefore a gentle sight-seeing trip, but calls for a reasonable standard of asceticism, discipline and self-control on the part of the pilgrim. Most of the tiny island is covered by a large domed church where sermons are preached and the pilgrims can pray and meditate.

The voyage to the island is now confined to a short if sometimes rather bumpy trip in large lifeboats, and air-conditioned charabancs bring the pilgrims from Dublin, but once they travelled by long and gradual stages stopping off at guesthouses on the islands of the Way of the Saints, their heads doubled almost to their knees in the bottom of the narrow cots. Doubtless the new means of travel is infinitely more comfortable, but what a lot they miss on the way!

Chapter 17

ATLANTIC ISLAND

AFTER exploring such a multitude of lake islands we decided to round off our voyage by visiting Aran Mor which is a large sea island in the Atlantic, off the western coast. So on one of those especially Irish days when short showers of rain run across the countryside followed by brief spells of hot sunshine, we drove over the moors and dropped down to the little city of Donegal which clings to the bank of its estuary like an elderly limpet toning in with the rocks and countryside around.

Beyond Donegal we entered a land which has been dominated and savaged by milleniums of Atlantic gales and wherever we glimpsed the sea it was in a tempestuous mood. Tall green breakers stacked behind each other came racing shorewards, thundered on the rocks and burst like explosions, scattering white needles of spray twenty and thirty feet into the sky. Alongside the quay at Burtonport we found a sturdy and broad-beamed fishing smack with a bow slanted high to ride the Atlantic breakers. After passing the two tall beacons north of Rutland Island we met the open sea and began to punch into the long rollers which were racing landwards and were made more savage by the rocks and shallows. The spray swept over our heads in broad sheets, but though it was rough the movement of the ship was far more comfortable than the bucking of the *Mary Ann* among the shorter and sharper waves on the lakes. Half an hour later the mainland had sunk to a thin line along the horizon in the east and high above us loomed the tall bulk of Aran with dozens of whitewashed cottages dotted along the landward side like gulls sheltering from the prevailing American winds.

Aran Mor, the Great Aran, should not be confused with the Aran Islands which we had seen in Galway Bay, which are linked to the mainland by a steamer service. Aran Mor is the largest of the sea islands of Ireland, rising 750 feet almost sheer from the breakers in some places and once containing a

198

population of near a thousand – now much diminished by emigration.

When we had moored at the quay we humped our cases up the hill towards the inn, but even half a mile inland the air was filled with the insidious voice of the sea, a persistent quavering rustle which is the eternal background music for life on this rugged outcrop of rock. Through and over it all ran that other element, the unending voice of the wind rising and falling through varying notes of intensity. At Leabgarrow a few Scots pines struggled for survival in the hollow beside the inn, their heads seemingly severed at the precise point where they rose from cover to meet the thrust of the gales, but at the other little village of Illion no trees had managed to survive.

At first we were surprised to find so many houses clustered along the mountainside and still inhabited for we wondered how so many people could earn a living on an island where only three or four fishing boats were anchored out in the bay. Later we learned that some of the people living in these cottages were wealthy enough, and had acquired considerable sums of capital from various employments abroad, often from running bars in Chicago and other prosperous American cities.

The landlord spoke of the relentless toll of the population which the Atlantic had taken down the years, though it seemed that fewer were lost through deep-sea fishing than in the tricky passage to and from the mainland. Not so long ago nineteen people set out for Burtonport when the sea was not even, by local standards, very rough, but they were too many for a small boat and all were drowned except one man who managed to cling to the timbers supporting his own father until he could hold him no more. Such was the greatest calamity of recent years, but there is a small craft, a cross between a punt and a dinghy which the islanders use to get to and from their fishing vessels and sometimes row to the mainland. After a glass or two on a stormy night one lad may challenge another to go back to Aran with him in one of these tiny craft, even though it is blowing up towards a gale. A few days later the remnants of their clothing may be found washed ashore thirty or forty miles away, for the sea is the savage ruler of this unrelenting coastline and few are skilled enough to challenge its dictatorship with impunity.

Though the islanders mostly speak Gaelic to each other a natural tolerance induces them to use English to strangers, and they have to be bi-lingual if they are thinking of emigrating or working abroad for a while. They speak it well enough, though softly, as though a mist from the waters had crept up into the bones of the language.

About four o'clock the next morning we were woken up by a series of ear-splitting explosions which shattered against the window-panes and filled the room with reverberations rather like a stick of bombs, but a little higher in pitch. The very idea of being blown up on Aran Mor seemed so remote that although I thought of getting up and asking what had happened, drowsiness soon won and I sank back fondly imagining that atomic explosions would normally make rather more noise than that. Various other explanations ran through my mind: I thought of old mines swept on to the rocks by the gale which was lashing by outside, or could it, I wondered, having recently heard a vivid and hilarious description of his wartime service in it from Patrick Campbell, could it possibly be the night exercises of the Irish Navy?

At breakfast the conundrum was solved simply enough when a fellow guest explained that the bombardment came from rockets fired to call the lifeboat crew from their homes. It seemed that a small fishing smack was in distress with a broken-down engine and was drifting out into the long Atlantic rollers some seventy-five miles beyond Sligo Bay. During Hitler's war a lifeboat was stationed at Sligo, but in peacetime funds no longer support it and the Aran boat now has to cover a considerable stretch of that treacherous coastline.

Later that morning we climbed up and over Frenchman's Hill to challenge the wind in full force, and close to the summit of the island we found a brown mountain tarn about a quarter of a mile long and well stocked with Rainbow trout.

"Rainbow trout in Ireland?" our fellow guest had asked us rhetorically at breakfast, "Never a one!" He leaned confidentially across the table towards us. "D'ye know what happened when they tried to put Rainbow trout in the other lakes? They arl committed suicide! Dived straight down to the bottom, stuck their noses in the mud, and when they drained one of those lakes they found the skilletons stickin' up out of the bottom, all tails and backbones!"

Concluding his horrific account he attributed this curious distaste for living in Ireland to some chemical in the water which affected the Rainbow more than any other species, though he thought that they stood a chance of surviving on Aran.

The wind was cutting us so hard that we paused only to peer briefly over the cliff on the precipitous seaward side and scan the horizon as though hoping to catch a glimpse of what they call on Aran "the next parish, in America", but we saw only the marching waves advancing and the lighthouse poised above the deep caves where the seals come to breed. There the stones on the cliff under our feet were crumbling and dangerous, the fishermen dare not use guns to reduce their numbers, for fear of bringing the rock down like bursting shells, while few will venture in with clubs, so the place remains sacrosanct.

Though it was late in the afternoon when we left the island we never learned whether the lifeboat made its rescue safely and found the Sligo smack. The breakers hurled us back towards the mainland more swiftly than we had come, and a dead seal floated past, belly uppermost in the waves. The skipper told us that the fishing had not been good that year, foreign vessels were poaching deep into Irish waters and the seals were taking a more than usually severe toll. As we emerged from the heavy seas into the smoother water among the inner islands we suddenly saw the head of a small terrier dog swimming gamely through the sea towards the mainland, but when I suggested hauling it aboard I was told that it belonged to a crofter on one of these islands, and apparently it thought nothing of swimming a mile to Burtonport and a mile back, sometimes partly against the tide.

After four months of our roving, nomadic life our voyaging was almost over and we drove gently back across Northern Ireland, visiting the great walls of Londonderry and Carrickfergus Castle. Down the east coast an explosion in boating has created dozens of new yacht clubs in recent years, and the modern Irishman is becoming almost as obsessed as the ancient monks of the Celtic Church with the magical business of messing about in boats.

The waterways on both sides of the border stand on the threshold of immense new developments and it was part of the design and achievement of our four-month-long voyage to show by our crossing of the country that most of these navigations are still open and functioning excellently. They offer so many thousands of miles of cruising that even half a century from now they will still be able to provide the visitor with that modicum of natural peace and tranquillity which will scarcely be available elsewhere in these islands.

When we reached the long quay at Belfast and boarded the ferry it was a clear, sunny autumn evening. Very gradually the ship slid away from her berth, seeming like a floating palace after the constrictions of the *Mary Ann*, and we dropped down the estuary with the ebbing tide. The lights of the coast winked up at us through the mist as though those ancient Druids were still at work weaving their spells and enchantments. While we leaned over the taffrail watching the wake glinting astern we recalled the warriors and the wizards, the winding lakes and the long wars and sieges. We thought of the monks, hermits and anchorites who had created those sanctuaries of peace and progress in their island abbeys. We remembered the pagan gods and their strange passing, the mountains rising steep from the rocky shores and the path of the tempting moon glittering across the lake waters of Lough Ree.

The last lights flickered out along the coast as we encountered the buck and swell of the sea, the Atlantic wind cut across and through us and it was time to go below.

"Ah well," as they once toasted each other in the great Assembly Hall of Tara, if you have troubled to read so far, why, *"here's to you, and may your shadow never grow less!"*

NOTES, ACKNOWLEDGEMENTS
AND BIBLIOGRAPHY

NOTE ONE

THIS work was originally designed as a straightforward travel book which would enable those who voyaged on the Shannon, Corrib and Erne navigations to obtain an insight into the history as well as the scenery of these lakes and islands. But we had the empirical advantage of actually travelling over considerable distances in much the same way as the earlier inhabitants of the country, and this perhaps more than any other factor contributed to some original archaeological theories which added a new and fascinating dimension to my researches. As I was not anxious to include footnotes in the text the following elucidation may serve as a guide to those who are interested in this aspect of the subject.

The Way of the Saints

The ancient highway called the Slige Mor or Great West Road ran from Tara to the Shannon and on to the Galway end of the Corrib Navigation, and was clearly a trade route between the kingdoms for merchandise, cattle and slaves; it may well have been the route travelled by the youthful Patrick on his way to tend the sheep of his Druid master in County Mayo. At or near Clonmacnois and Galway the road must have linked up with the water transport of cots and coraghs, and goods would have been carried by boat to and from the densely populated lakes and islands. It seemed necessary to suggest a name which time will reject or corroborate, so I have called these water routes The Way of the Saints because it was these early ascetics who left the most outstanding extant memorials in their monastic churches, abbeys and round towers. The inaccessibility of their island sites combined with the Irishman's inherent veneration for ancient monuments has preserved these unique groups of buildings in some places almost intact. A close continuity was

205

maintained with the old Druidic faith and with some of its traditions for the new foundations were almost all sited on earlier cultic centres, the high standard of asceticism was maintained and even the Druidic tonsure was adopted by the new occupants.

The Neale Stones

In view of the evidence submitted here it would be difficult to maintain that the carved stones called the *Gods of the Neale* were of pagan origin, and I am encouraged in this opinion by Lord Kilmaine who tells me that he does not believe that such carvings could date from the pre-Christian era in Ireland. I feel reasonably convinced of the general accuracy of my interpretation of the stones but it may be considered that their title, The *Gods* of the Neale, is not very appropriate in the light of the present evidence and that they should perhaps be called the Kilmaine Stones, or the Neale Stones, in honour of their preservation at a time when so much was being destroyed.

The Wild Boar

One hopes that the theories put forward on the hunting and sacrifice of the wild boar will help to reveal more about the Druidic worship of the sun, its worldly associate fire, and the god Manannan Mac Lir. The theology of the hog has taken on different dimensions and should be of value in assessing the constantly recurring symbol of the boar in Celtic art and religion.

There is powerful and logical evidence that the Celts were hunters long before they were herdsmen and cultivators, and the ritual significance of the fire boar would spring naturally from their hunting propensities. Later, pigs were kept on islands, which was a sensible arrangement because they were less likely to stray and were readily available for sacrifice as well as for sustenance, hence the number of islands called Muckinish, or Pig Island, on these lakes. The processes of sacrifice lie at the very roots of our racial development and involved the essential acts of propitiating the gods or seeking benefits from them, the

206

most important being the omnipotent sun and the magical moon without whose benevolent influence they believed that life would surrender to the forces of darkness, storm and waste. Hence the ritual burning of the forest boar at Tara and elsewhere would have ensured the return of the sun, or the welcoming of it at their feasts of Samain and Beltine. It follows naturally from this that a hunting aristocracy would sacrifice what it valued most highly, the *torc caille*, or wild boar, which has a far more delicate flavour than ordinary pork.

Manannan Mac Lir is perhaps the most fascinating product of the Druidic mind for he has the supreme Socratic virtue of portending certain aspects of Christianity. In lecturing I have for some years dealt with the classical precursors of the Christian ethic but it is intriguing to find that we possess a harbinger of our moral theology so much nearer home in our own Celtic folklore : this is a subject on which I hope to be able to produce some further comments shortly. Manannan's association with the wild boar was due to his duty of providing from his magical islands the pork Feast of Age, which ensured the immortality of the Tuatha, or gods, and he was therefore an extremely important member of the divine hierarchy – sufficiently important to have his parallels in the other Celtic lands of Gaul and Britain.

I base the theory that the carved figures on Manannan are boars, not only on the cloven hoofs but also on the curious line running down to the ham and on the fact that I can trace no other Celtic deity associated so closely, or so importantly, with a specific animal of this kind. Many writers have suggested that the mouths of these creatures on the White Island statue are beak-like, but they appear to me to be rather bulbous as though the sculptor was either attempting to portray the area around a tusk, or else depicting the mouth hanging open. The God of Euffigneix has only *one* boar carved on his stomach.

White Island

The recognition of the other gods on White Island must remain somewhat tenuous suggestions only, though I am reasonably convinced by the piper and his chanter. Here again I would suggest that the most constructive approach is to link up the symbols on each of the figures with whatever clues we possess from Celtic mythology, for the symbolism is clearly straightforward and uncomplicated. Most of the figures have sockets set into their heads which were, I believe, originally intended for supporting golden crowns or headpieces, and the sculptures would have been rather more impressive and dignified with the gold and perhaps precious jewels glinting on them. Their odd semi-crouched position is clearly a debased form of the cross-legged seated position associated with the carvings of Celtic deities at the cultic centre of Roquerteuse in France. Like the Romans the Celts were more given to reclining than to sitting, so that if mythology in Ireland could have been descended from Hinduism as in the case of Moling, so these seated figures may owe some debt to yoga. From what little we know of Druidic ritual it would certainly not have been lacking in asceticism.

The Eastern origin of the Celts was firmly established by J. C. Prichard's philological study published in 1831, which emphasized the link between Gaelic and Sanskrit. Now that researches in mythology are confirming this view there can be no doubt that Celtic art forms, like the figure on the Gundestrup silver cauldron, owe much to Indian influences. Most modern scholars are inclined to believe that the worship of the snake and the sun was of Egyptian origin, and was carried into India by Aryan invaders from the Eastern Mediterranean. It could therefore be one of the more curious ironies of history that servants of the British Raj returned to India to hunt wild boar over country once traversed by their nomadic and pastoralist ancestors.

One can hardly accept the current date of the eighth century as probable for the White Island figures, even allowing for the late survival of pagan practices. The creative element in Druidism must have been waning considerably by the late sixth century, but the transition from pagan to Christian sculpture implies an even earlier date, for we must remember that Whithorn Abbey extended a powerful pre-Patrician missionary influence over this area and doubtless found sympathetic support from the devotees of Manannan.

NOTE TWO
The Devil God

In demythologizing the Devil, and tracing his origins back to Cernunnos the chthonic fertility god it is only just to point out that he was not in origin essentially evil, though certain aspects of his worship were evil by *later* ethical standards. I am indebted to Miss Anne Ross's Pagan Celtic Britain and her mention of this god as the "prototype for the horned, squatting, serpent-bearing Satan", though among Roman importations Pan, or Faunus as they called him, must also have had some slight influence in Britain; though not precisely commensurate these two gods do have marked similarities.

It should be noted that some authorities consider Rathcrogan a more likely burial place for Queen Maeve, while others deny that she is an historical character at all.

A very recent theory expounded by Professors N. Chadwick and M. Dillon suggests that Maeve embodied the concept of Sovereignty, and as such was "wooed" by successive Irish kings, though Mrs. Chadwick holds the view that Maeve was in origin an historical queen of Connaught. There is now no doubt that these ancient sagas of Ireland were once 'religious' works, rather akin to the Indian Vedas and to the Greek Myths explored by Mr. Robert Graves.

NOTE TWO

The Oral Tradition

The accusation that scholars have levelled at the Celtic monks of plots to write tall stories about the miracles of their patron saints in order to draw additional revenue from pilgrims, does perhaps have a small measure of truth in it, but has been much exaggerated. As Professor Rees hints in *Celtic Heritage* their main aim was to supersede the Druid mythology with an equally powerful Christian one, and to achieve this exercise in public relations they did not hesitate to adapt many of the best and tallest pagan legends and apply them to their own saints.

An incident in the early life of St. Moling serves as a splendid example of this process of grafting and adaptation. His pagan name was Tairchell, and as a young ordinand he decided to go on circuit to collect alms for his abbey, taking with him two wallets, a begging bowl and an ashen staff, but as he went his way he met the Evil Spectre surrounded by his diabolical henchmen. The Spectre challenged him and threatened to drive his spear through the saint's side, but Moling replied that he would crack the evil one's head open with his trusty staff. Then, thinking better of a rather uneven combat he used his wits and asked a boon, which was to be allowed to borrow three leaps, and when this was granted his first jump carried him so far that he seemed no larger than a crow in the distance. With the second leap he vanished altogether, and with the third he landed back on the wall of the monastic campus and bolted into the safety of the church, just before the thwarted demons could catch him.

Now the fascinating fact about this otherwise not very illuminating tale is that it has an almost precise parallel in the Indian *Ramayana* of the Hindus, where the god Vishnu overcomes the demon Bali with three borrowed leaps, and so gains possession of the earth, the atmosphere and the sky, sending Bali to the underworld in a fascinating takeover bid. Heaven alone knows down what long aeons and around what endless chains of camp fires that tale must have been repeated from mouth to mouth and held in memory after memory, before it came to be associated with the Abbot of St. Mullins on the estuary of the River Barrow! Moling and Vishnu represent the vital elements or gods of light and goodness, while the spectre and Bali are the gods of darkness and evil, for the Christian faith was not unique in evolving around the ancient concept of heaven and hell.

The whole point of an oral tradition is that it must contain rather startling facts if it is to be reasonably easily committed to memory, for before the introduction of writing man's memory had to serve as his library, archives and "bible". Naturally this tradition continued into the early Church which adapted and invented equally startling tales but linked them with its own saints, and martyrs. The extent to which the old religion lingered on as it were under the skin of the new is perhaps best illustrated in St. Patrick himself. It was no coincidence that when he returned with the sailors to Britain and spent perhaps the worst night of his life dreaming that Satan was descending on him like a rock, he should call out in his need not to the Christian god but to Helias, the deity of the sun :

> But whence came it into my mind, ignorant as I am to call upon Helias? And meanwhile I saw the sun rise in the sky, and while I was shouting Helias! Helias! with all my might, suddenly the splendour of that sun fell on me and freed me of all misery.

His cries, if understood, would certainly have surprised his pagan companions after his refusal to take a pagan oath. Patrick was far too honest to exclude this incident from his *Confession* but it was really perfectly natural that even the best Christian who had just escaped from slavery in a land of sun worship should have made, in his sleeping subconscious, an appeal to the god of the sun when the Devil was descending on him, for the old faith lay not far beneath the skin. It could even be argued that the saint's nightmare arose in part from the feast of roast pork recently killed by his companions after their enforced period of fasting, and that sun and the sacrifice of pigs were naturally linked in his mind through his personal knowledge of the *torc caille*. The original work is very well worth reading, and has been published by Longmans, Green & Co., with translation and notes by Mr. Ludwig Bieler. In that work will be found a direct translation of the famous Lorica and it is interesting to see how much Mrs. Alexander's version, used in Chapter II, has added to the original.

It will also be interesting to see how long the Bury theories of Patrick, at present so deeply entrenched in Irish school textbooks, will take to decline before the far more accurate view of Professor Hanson. It was not in Armagh that Patrick tended sheep, and he did not visit Gaul!

ACKNOWLEDGEMENTS

I am considerably indebted to the following people who have made the completion of this work possible. The first tribute should be to my wife, who endured the hardships of a long and gruelling voyage in a small boat and whose archaeological library and advice have both been invaluable. Mr. Colm O'Lochlainn of Dublin has willingly and tolerantly assisted me with many points of scholarship. Mr. John Switzer of Enniskillen, General Manager of W. Trimble Ltd., publishers of the *Impartial Reporter* has aided me generously during several years of research and has helped my many requests for information. The details of some of the Erne islands have been made more accurate by Mrs. Mary Rogers' kind permission to include some factual material from her *Prospect of Erne*. Cynthia and the late Col. Harry Rice aided me with valuable notes and information on the Shannon, and Lord Kilmaine with a fund of local historical detail on The Neale House and estate. Mr. D. B. McNeill has aided me with expert advice and notes on the lake steamers, and the Rev. J. K. Byrom with invaluable books and encouragement. Our voyage on the Erne was made much more comfortable by Mr. and Mrs. Mark Hughes, the hospitable owners of the good ship *Blink*. While John and Betty Williams made the start of our journeying possible Mr. and Mrs. Walter Braidwood made its termination so much pleasanter than it would otherwise have been.

To Mr. Henry Burke of Ballinamallard we owed a special debt for enabling us to visit the Erne, and the Rev. G. P. Irvine for the use of his private docking facilities with the aid of Mr. T. Balfour. Among others who helped us generously were Mr. Sean MacBride, the former Foreign Minister of Eire, Major Henry Cavendish Butler, Mr. Gordon Clark, Commander Crichton, the Rev. Thomas Egan, the Rev. Peadar Livingstone, the Rev. Oliver Kennedy, Mr. Alf MacLochlainn of the National Library,

NOTE TWO

Mr. Herbert Morel, Mr. Desmond Moore, Mr. and Mrs. Horatio Darby, the Rev. Kenneth Riley, Mr. Mervyn Dane, Mr. P. V. B. Jebb, Mr. David Wolfenden and Mr. John Phillips, Dr. E. MacLysaght, Mr. and Mrs. J. Hannavig, Mr. T. L. H. Huston, N.I. Tourist Board, and the members of the Lough Erne Yacht Club.

I am indebted to the Warden, staff and students of Brasted College for the encouragement which they have given me in undertaking this research.

The extracts from the poetry of W. B. Yeats are included by arrangement with Mr. M. B. Yeats and Macmillan & Co. Ltd., publishers of *The Collected Poetry of W. B. Yeats.* Those not acknowledged in the text come from *The Ragged Wood, Meditations in Time of Civil War* and *Nineteen Hundred and Nineteen* (the last two from *Selected Poetry* by A. N. Jeffares.)

The satirical verse and the rowing song of Columbanos are extracts from Ireland. *Harbinger of The Middle Ages* by Mr. Ludwig Bieler, and are included by the generous permission of the Oxford University Press. The extract from *The Abbey That Refused to Die* is included by kind permission of the Poet Laureate and the Rev. Thomas Egan. The lines from Shan Bullock's *Mors Et Vita* are included by the generous permission of his daughter, Mrs. E. M. Elson.

For permission to use their photographs for reproduction in this work, acknowledgement is made to the following: Mr Mervyn Dane, Mrs. Mary Rogers, Bord Failte, the photographic library of the Northern Ireland Tourist Board, the *Connacht Tribune*, the Ulster Museum and the Musée des Antiquités Nationales, St. Germain-en-Laye at Paris. The Manannan photograph comes from the Welch Collection.

BIBLIOGRAPHY

The investigations connected with this work having involved some seven years of research; it would not be possible to include in this list every one of the books and papers consulted so that the following is rather a general guide to the inquiring reader than a complete bibliography of each relevant subject.

BIELER, LUDWIG: *The Works of St. Patrick*, The Newman Press, Maryland, U.S.A., and Longmans Green & Co., London.
Ireland. Harbinger of the Middle Ages, Oxford University Press, London.

CHADWICK, NORA K.: *Celtic Britain*, Thames and Hudson, London.

DELANY, V. T. H. and D. R.: *The Canals of the South of Ireland*, David and Charles, Newton Abbott, Devon.

DILLON, MYLES and CHADWICK, NORA: *The Celtic Realms*, Weidenfeld and Nicolson, London.

EGAN, REV. T. A.: *Ballintubber Abbey*, booklet published privately by the author.

FAHY, J. A.: *The Glory of Cong*, published privately by the author.

HANSON, R. P. C.: *St. Patrick*, Oxford University Press, London.

H.M. STATIONERY OFFICE: *Ancient Monuments of Northern Ireland*, two volumes.

KENDRICK, T. D.: *The Druids*, Frank Cass, London.

LEASK, H. G.: *Irish Castles and Castellated Houses*, Dundalgan Press, Dundalk, Eire.

LOWRY-CORRY, LADY DOROTHY: *Statute at White Island, Ulster Journal of Archaeology*, No. 22, 1959.

MACALISTER, R. A. S.: *Tara: A Pagan Sanctuary of Ancient Ireland*, Charles Scribner's Sons, New York.

MCCUTCHEON, W. A.: *The Canals of the North of Ireland*, David & Charles, Newton Abbott, Devon.

MCNEILL, D. B.: *Coastal Passenger Steamers and Inland Navigations in Northern Ireland*, Ulster Museum and Art Gallery, Belfast.

MASON, T. H.: *The Islands of Ireland*, Mercier Press, Cork.

OFFICIAL GUIDE: *Enniskillen*.

BIBLIOGRAPHY

O'LOCHLAINN, COLM : *More Irish Street Ballads*, Three Candles Press, Dublin.

PIGGOTT, STUART : *The Druids*, Thames and Hudson, London.

PLUMMER, C.: *Lives of the Irish Saints*, Oxford University Press, London.

POWELL, T. G. E. : *The Celts*, Thames and Hudson, London.

PRAEGER, LOUIS : *The Way That I Went*, Hodges and Figgis, Dublin.

REES, ALWYN and REES, BRINLEY; *Celtic Heritage, Ancient Tradition in Ireland and Wales*, Thames and Hudson, London.

RICE, HARRY: *Thanks for the Memory*, Athlone Printing Co., Athlone.

The Islands of Lough Ree. Private Notes.

ROGERS, MARY: *Prospect of Erne*, Fermanagh Field Club.

ROLT, L. T. C.: *Green and Silver*, Allen and Unwin, London.

ROSS, ANNE : *Pagan Celtic Britain*, Routledge and Kegan Paul, London.

SIMPSON, W., DOUGLAS : *The Historical Saint Columba*, Oliver and Boyd, London.

SQUIRE, CHARLES, *Celtic Myth and Legend, Poetry and Romance*, Gresham Publishing Co. Ltd., London.

WILDE, SIR WILLIAM R.: *Loch Coirib*, The Three Candles Press, Dublin.

WILLIAMS, HUGH : *Christianity in Early Britain*, Oxford University Press, London.

For a general travel book on the waterways of the Republic south of Athlone and including The Grand Canal, The Barrow Navigation and the Shannon from Athlone to the Estuary, cf. Part II of *Voyage In a Bowler Hat* by Hugh Malet.

215

INDEX

INDEX

Saints and Loughs are entered under names, not titles.

INDEX

INDEX